NEW GRAPHIC DESIGN
ART & CREATIVITY
GRAPHICS

LINKS

Edition 2012

Author: Dimitris Kottas
Graphic design & production: Cuboctaedro
Collaborator: Oriol Vallés
Text: Contributed by the architects, edited by Naomi Ferguson

© LinksBooks
Jonqueres, 10, 1-5
08003 Barcelona, Spain
Tel.: +34-93-301-21-99
Fax: +34-93-301-00-21
info@linksbooks.net
www.linksbooks.net

NEW GRAPHIC DESIGN
ART & CREATIVITY
GRAPHICS

LINKS

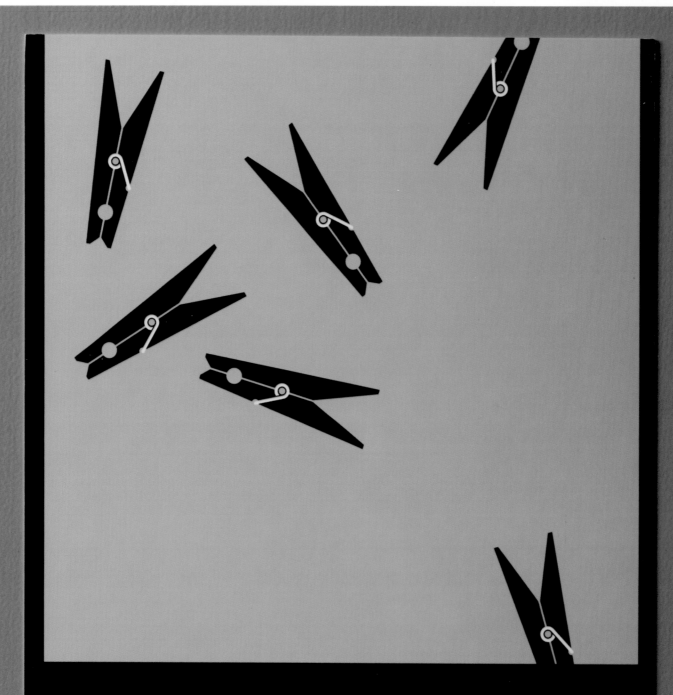

Tuesday, September 14, 2010
10AM
EXIT ART
475 Tenth Avenue at 36th Street
New York
R.S.V.P.
nicole@bradburylewis.com
BY INVITATION ONLY
www.karenwalker.com

SHISEIDO
Bumble and bumble.

Contents

This book brings together a selection of graphic design projects realized for art institutions, creative professionals and companies, as well as graphic designers' own publicity projects and personal investigation projects. What distinguishes clients from the world of art and the creative industries is that they are usually interested in being at the forefront of innovation in visual design. Far from the conservative efficiency and trust that have to be conveyed in a corporate project, these projects have to show daring, originality and innovation. Designers can allow themselves even greater creative freedom when they are also the client. With no restrictions other than those that the designer gives himself, such projects represent the opportunity to realize a "dream project", unleashing the full force of designers' ideas and talent.

Experimentation with typography, format and printing tehcniques, unusual and provocative uses of images and innovative layouts are all encouraged under such conditions. The designer is able to follow the strictest order or create the most daring formal designs stretching the limits of readability or usefulness.

For these reasons, the field of graphic design for the art and creative industries constitutes the perfect context for the emergence of avant-garde tendencies. In this book you will find some of the most well known contemporary designers such as Brogen Averill, Heydays, Method and Mind Design together with younger designers that will constitute tomorrow's vanguard in graphic design. Any designer interested in learning about the most advanced tendencies and ideas in graphic design will find this book to be an invaluable source of inspiration.

Graphic identity for the Norwegian creative agency Dist. Focusing on the creative processes of the designers as reflected in material such as rough sketches from their drawing boards, Anti combined this material with a strict and edgy logo signature and a grid template that represented the designers as a strange cult that follows a strict set of rules to reach the creative outcome. To top it all, Anti created the world's largest business card. Featured in the Guinness World Records, it is sure to leave a massive impression when someone carries it into a meeting room!

Art Direction: Kjetil Wold
Graphic Design: Martin Stousland
Photo: Stian Andersen

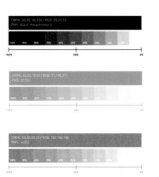

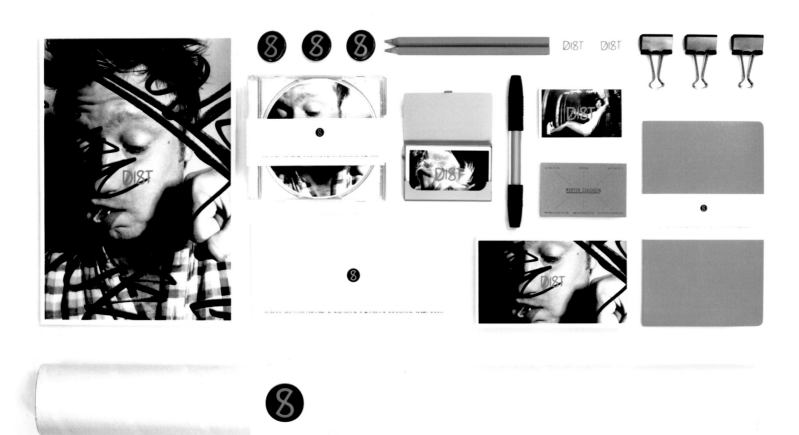

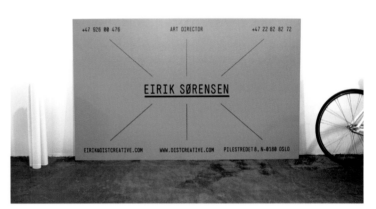

Apfel Zet

Illustrative

Corporate design for the annual illustration festival, 2006-2011. Based on a pencil logo and the basic printing colours cyan, magenta, yellow and black, Apfel Zet developed a pure design with overtones of the Swiss typography of Josef Müller Brockmann and the Ulm school of design.

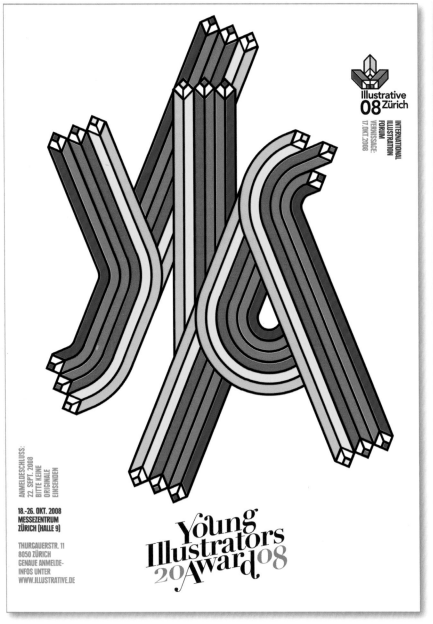

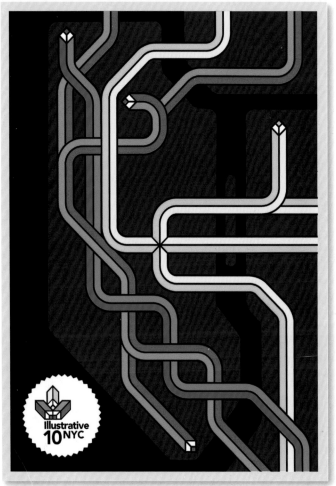

Illustrative 10 Berlin

10 Berlin

INTERNATIONAL
ILLUSTRATION
FORUM

01.11.-16.11.2010

Villa Elisabeth
Invalidenstr. 3
10115 Berlin

info@illustrative.de
www.illustrative.de

Plotki Magazin

Cover and editorial design for the 7th issue, "nightshift", of the monothematic magazine "Plotki" about Eastern Europe, 2006. The cover design was inspired by Chris Ware and Hergé.

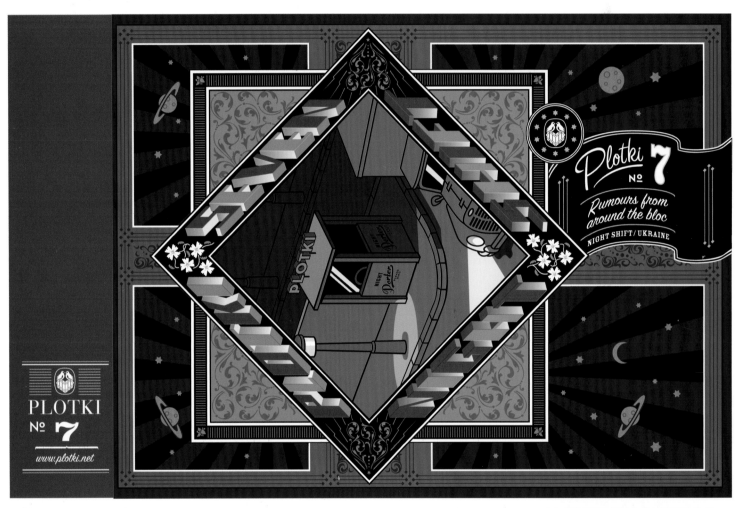

Objects

Editorial design for a magazine about Illustration and Neo Craft, 2009.

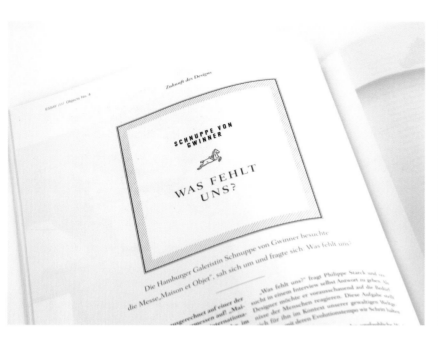

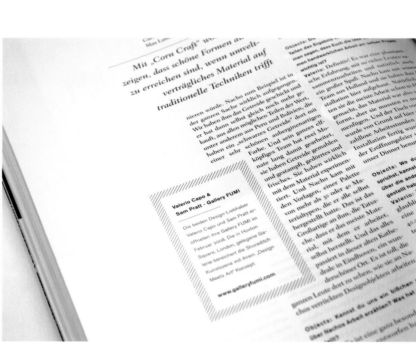

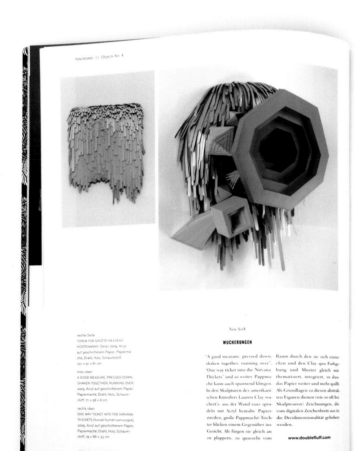

Singapore International Photography Festival (SIPF)

The Singapore International Photography Festival is an international biennial for the advancement and appreciation of photography. The 2nd SIPF was intended to serve as a platform for Southeast Asian photographers to showcase their works alongside their international counterparts. The festival identity design stemmed from the idea of "putting together a show". The key visual uses a stack of prints much like a curator might use to select works for an exhibition. The stack of photographs teases viewers with what they might see when they attend the festival. This theme is then extended to the invitation card and the programme booklet. For the booklet, the programme listings and details were laid out to resemble post-it notes and pieces of notes overlaid on the images. Photography and camera related festival T-shirts to be sold during the festival were also designed by Asylum.

Creative Director: Chris Lee
Designer: Yong
Photographer: Lumina Photography

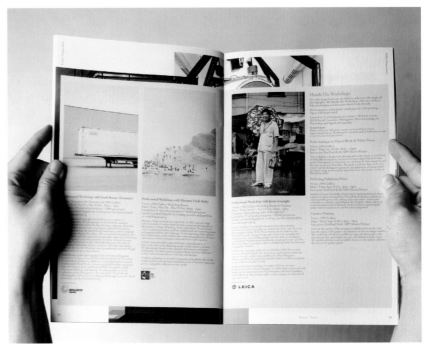

Lleida Literary Awards

Inspired by the image of the spines of books on a shelf and the comma, Atipus developed the visual image for the Lleida Literary Awards festival. They defined a carefully controlled color palette which was used to differentiate the various elements.

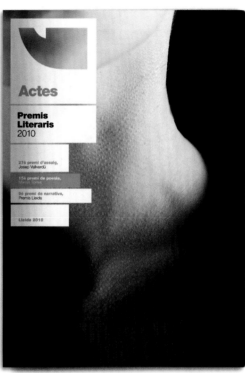

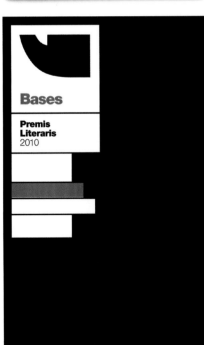

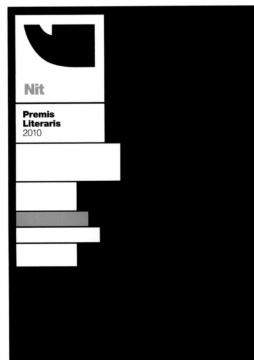

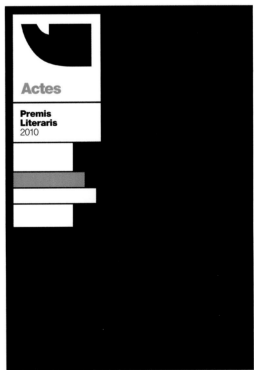

Atipus

Atipus

With the design of their own business cards and collateral, the Barcelona-based design studio, Atipus, wanted to transmit the importance of details in their design philosophy.

They worked with two elements: adhesive labels that allowed them to personalize the different media and printing "errors" as graphic features that gave a distinctive character to the stationery. Each business card is a pamphlet bearing a portrait photo of the designer, which is folded to the traditional size of a business card and sealed with an adhesive label. The recipient is forced to break the seal in order to see inside. They work as little surprise objects.

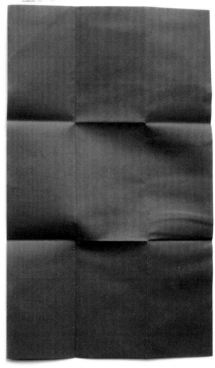

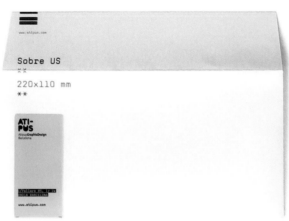

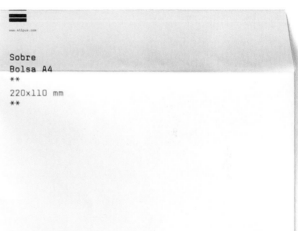

Brogen Averill

Karen Walker

Invitation to the presentation of the Karen
Walker "Perfect Day" collection in New York.

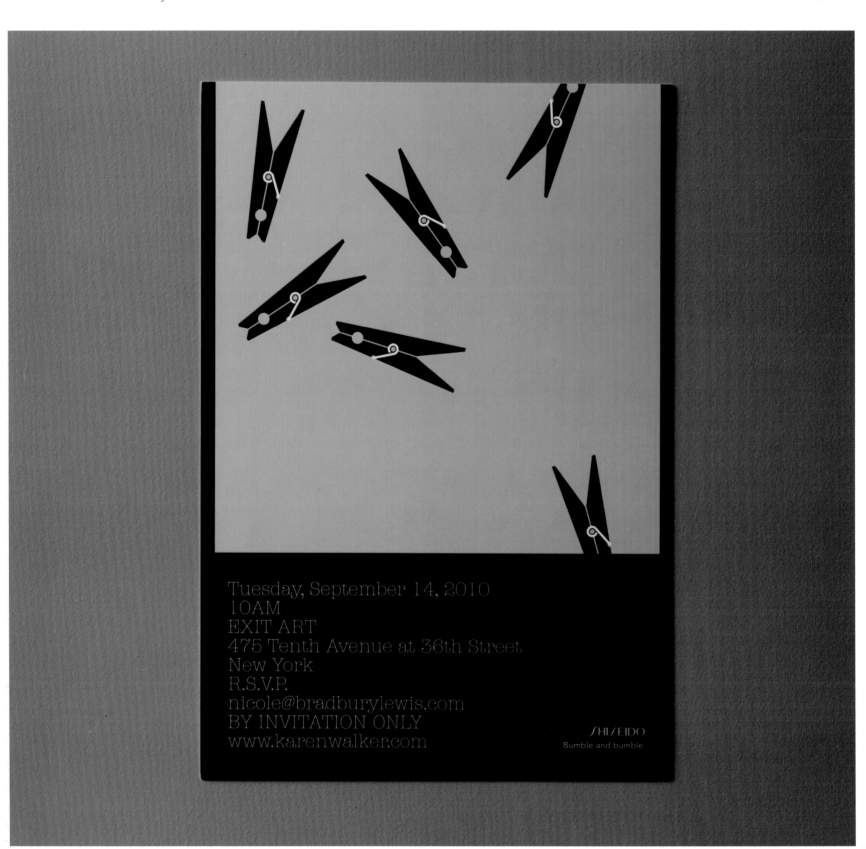

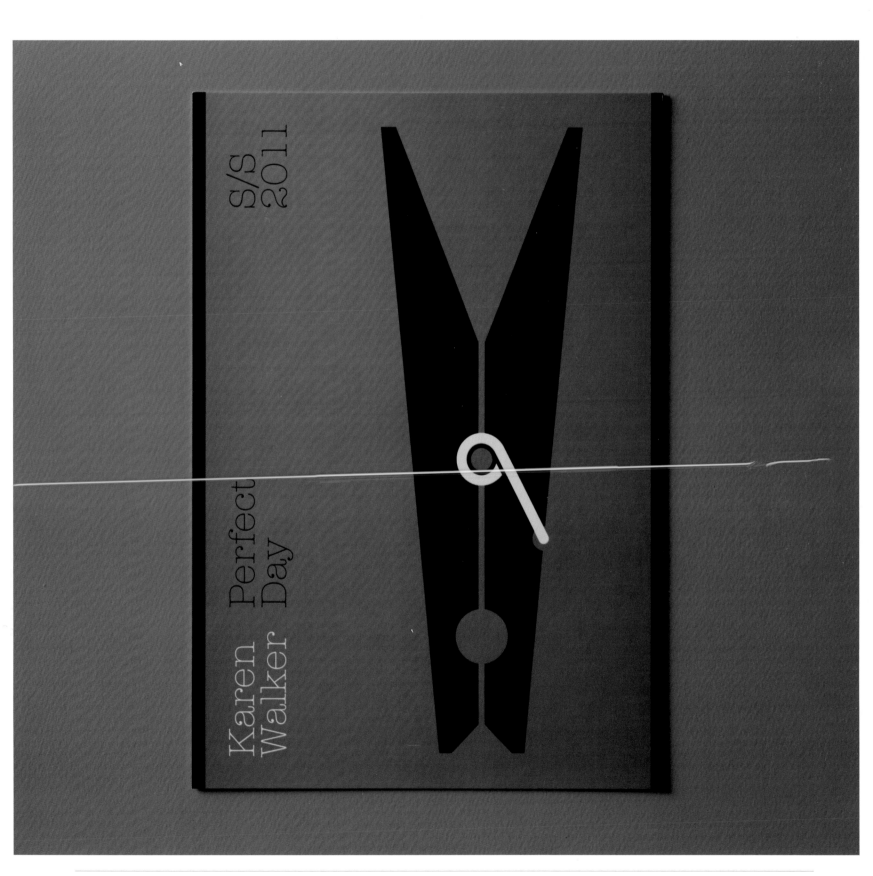

Edgar Bąk

Krakow Literature Days

Visual identity for the Krakow literature festival. The principal theme of the festival was the human in the city, so the design imitates the aesthetics of traffic signs, signposts and the language of the city in forms and in colors (pure black and fluorescent pantone 805c). Design package included four different posters, a leaflet and a book cover.

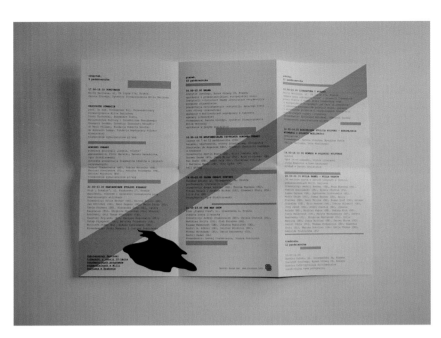

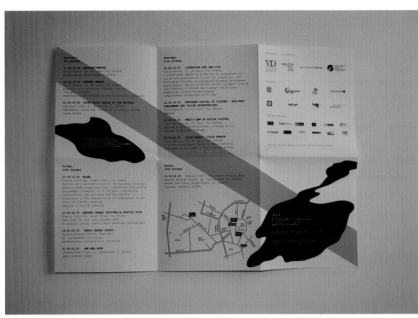

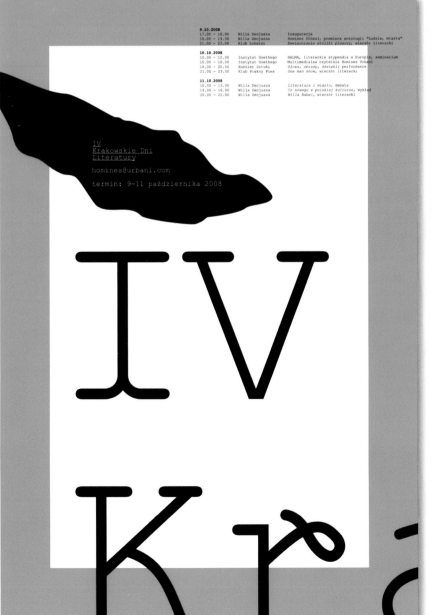

Edgar Bąk

Photomonth in Krakow

Ongoing work on the visual identity of the biggest Polish photo festival. The design was successfully reduced to a specific font and colour, which were then adapted for each subsequent edition of the event.

MIESIĄC
FOTOGRAFII
W KRAKOWIE

GOŚĆ SPEC-
JALNY: CZECHY
SPECIAL GUEST:
CZECH REPUBLIC

czescy klasycy czerni i bieli/ młode pokolenie/
najciekawsi artyści współcześni/ fotografia
a reżim/ awangarda i prowincja/ Kolář, Tichý,
David, Mancuska, Kovanda, Othová.../
Czech classics of black & white/ young generation/
the most interesting contemporary artists/
photography and regime/ vanguard and province/
Kolář, Tichý, David, Mancuska, Kovanda, Othová...

PROGRAM TEMATYCZNY:
PAMIĘĆ PRZETWARZANA
THEMATIC PART
MEMORY PROCESSED

PROGRAM OFF:
MY[PHOTO]SPACE,
PORTFOLIO REVIEW,
PHOTOSTREET

drugie życie archiwum/ publiczne vs.
prywatne/ fotografia a Holokaust /
Poznań 56' z ukrycia/ Witkacy, WeeGee,
Yamamoto, Odermatt.../ the second life
of archives/ public vs. private/ act, facts
& internet/ photography and Holocaust/
democratic demonstrations backstage/
Witkacy, WeeGee, Yamamoto, Odermatt...

www.photomonth.com

otwarcie: 8 maja
wernisaże: 8—10 maja
wydarzenia: 9—17 maja
opening night 8th of May,
opening weekend
8th-10th of May

W KRAKOWIE
MAJ

SPOTKANIA, DYSKUSJE,
PROJEKCJE, WARSZTATY
MEETINGS, DISCUSSIONS,
SCREENINGS, WORKSHOPS

5—31
MAJA
5—31
OF MAY

PROGRAM OFF:
MY[PHOTO]SPACE,
PORTFOLIO REVIEW,
PHOTOSTREET

drugie życie archiwum/ publiczne vs.
prywatne/ fotografia a Holokaust /
Poznań 56' z ukrycia/ Witkacy, WeeGee,
Yamamoto, Odermatt.../ the second life
of archives/ public vs. private/ act, facts
& internet/ photography and Holocaust/
democratic demonstrations backstage/
Witkacy, WeeGee, Yamamoto, Odermatt...

35 wystaw, 100 artystów, 50 projektów
z całego świata/ uznani kuratorzy/
gwiazdy międzynarodowej fotografii/
przez cały maj, w całym Krakowie...
35 exhibitions, 100 artists, 50 projects
from all over the world/ best curators/
international stars of photography/
all May, whole Krakow...

2009

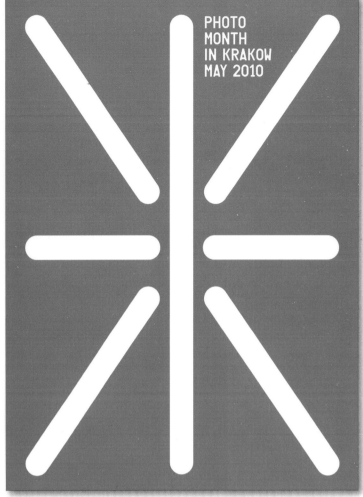

PHOTO
MONTH
IN KRAKOW
MAY 2010

MIESIĄC
FOTOGRAFII
W KRAKOWIE 2011
PHOTOMONTH
IN KRAKOW

ALIAS

13.05
—12.06

MIESIĄC
FOTOGRAFII
W KRAKOWIE
MAJ 2008

Quer – Symposium for Intercreativity

A three-day international symposium in March 2010 was dedicated to a pressing issue in the art, design and theatre worlds: how do different creative disciplines work together? What expectations do they have and what work models do they follow? Together with the designers Numen/for use, bauer – konzept & gestaltung developed a visual introduction to these topics and questions: a spatial walk-in installation made of transparent tape. Single strings concentrated in the middle of the old Odeon Theatre to form a sculpture which was used as a projection surface for an animation of the symposium's logo, as well as a stage for a dance performance. Referring to the installation, bauer developed a profound visual concept for the accompanying communication media, the screen design for the lectures and the homepage – all following the key principle of connecting lines.

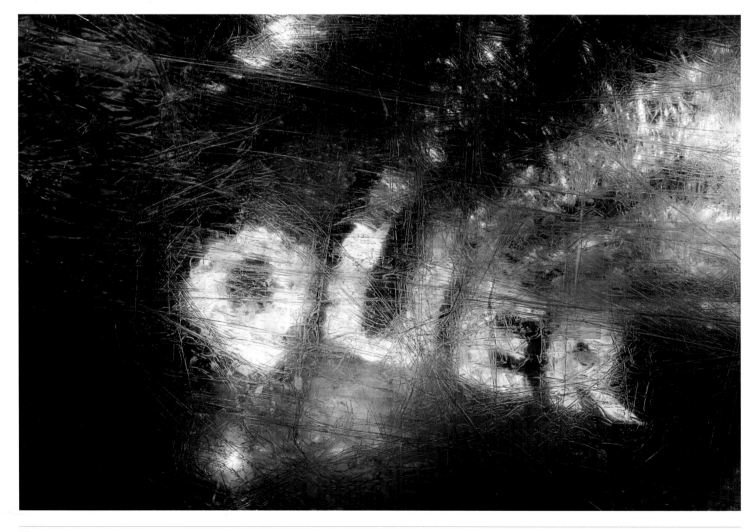

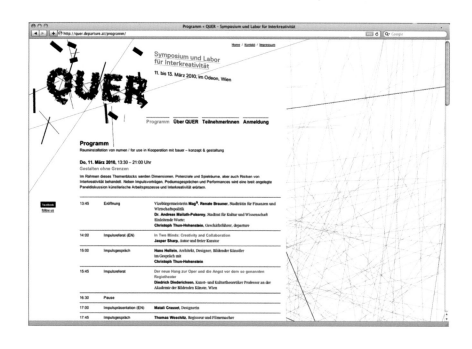

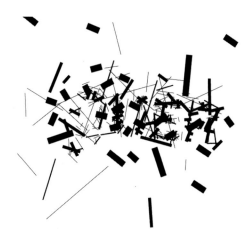

Sputnic Architektur

Architect Norbert Steiner is responsible for many vibrant architectural projects, and bauer – konzept & gestaltung developed the defining concept for his corporate visual identity. Part of the design was customised corporate font – called "Sputnic Breitfett" – which is applied in all communication media, such as image folders, posters, stationery and the website, all developed by bauer – konzept & gestaltung. The typeface was created specifically for this project and is a modern, incisive font, inspired by the romanian proverb *"Knotty timber requires sharp wedges."*

SPUTNIC ORIGINAL BREITFETT

30

„AUF EINEN GROBEN KLOTZ GEHŒRT EIN GROBER KEIL." RUSSISCHES SPRICHWORT

ABCDEFGHIJKLMNO PQRSTUVWXYYZ ÆŒŒŁŁ0123456789
.,;:!?…+*-–""''

Struggle for the City

Struggle for the City was the name of an inter-disciplinary exhibition about politics, the arts and everyday life in Austria during the 1920s and 1930s. bauer – konzept & gestaltung created the visual design of the exhibition, the communication media and accompanying catalogue, including a custom-designed font called "Reklame Stencil". The unique type-face was meant to shape and reinfirce the visual language of the show. The starting point for the design was the title block of the "Österreichische Reklame", a magazine for advertising art first published in 1926. Referring to the few existing capital letters, the rest of the alphabet was created with simple elements such as circles, triangles and rectangles. The result is an avantgardist, rhythmically balanced typeface with rounded corners and oscillating serifs: "Reklame Stencil". Once applied, it links the exhibition and the accompanying communication media with the zeitgeist of the 1930s.

Boccalatte

Bundanon Trust

Boccalatte have been working closely with Deborah Ely and her team at the Bundanon Trust for the last few years. The venue run by the trust is a wonderful, magical place for artists, writers and other creative professionals.

Art Direction: Suzanne Boccalatte
Annual Report Design: Martin Ford

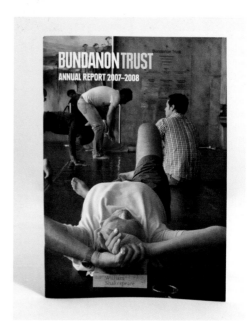

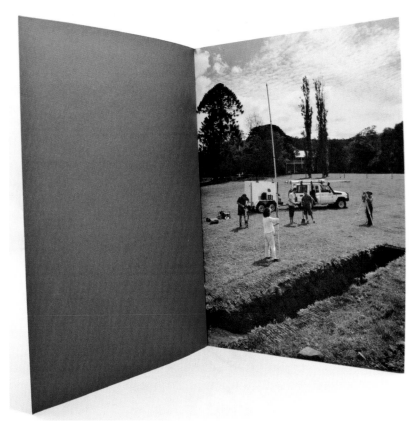

Sydney Design 2010

The Sydney Design 2010 theme was story-telling. Every design has a story, or at least the designers at Boccalatte believe it should. As part of a design process, conversations take place between the designer and the clients connecting ideas, desires and needs.

Sydney Design venues were plotted on a Google map reference with Powerhouse Museum as the starting point. Events branch out and connect to each other, playing with notions of social relationships, networks and narrative pathways. The overlapping lines and colours represent the depth, movement and connections that storytelling creates. These connections create virtual spaces and represent the wonderful variety of design fields whether graphics, architecture, industrial design, fashion or even origami.

A penchant for books shared by the designers at Boccalatte inspired them to translate the storytelling theme of the event into the produciton of a paperback book to accompany the festival. With a Penguin Classics paperback in mind, they designed the black & white book and organised its production.

Art Direction & Design: Suzanne Boccalatte
Illustration: Alexandra De Bonis
Client: Powerhouse Museum

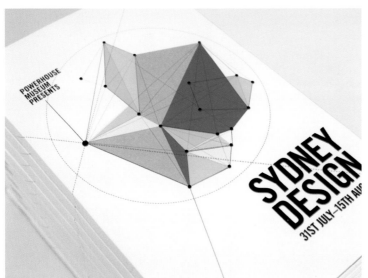

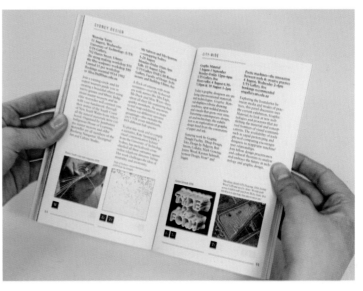

SantaMonica

Branding, integral graphic identity, promotional material and collaterals for SantaMonica, a Barcelona-based clothing brand.

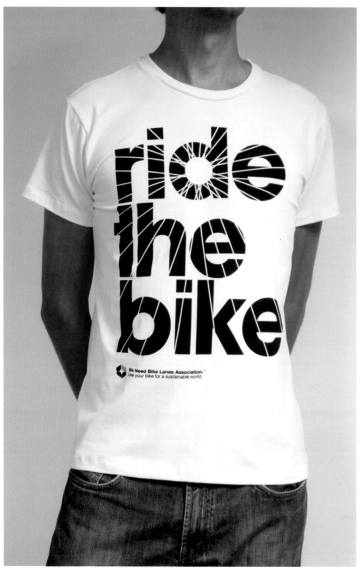

RUN FOR YOUR LIFE

Mies is More

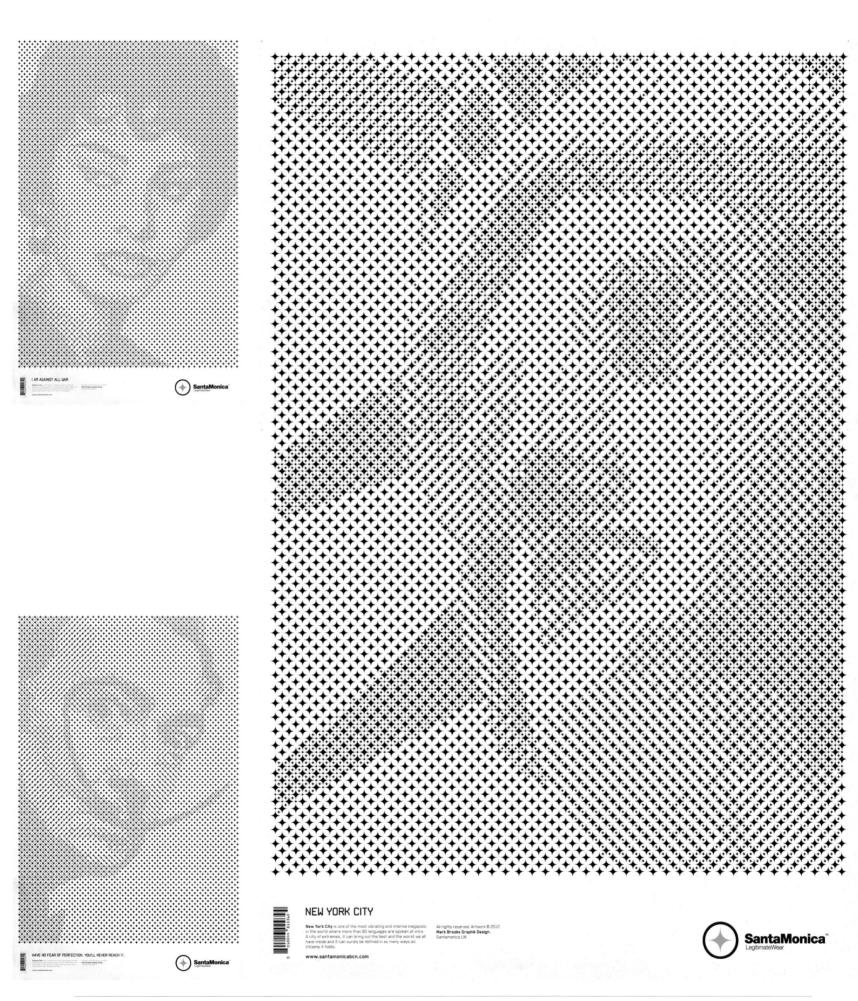

I AM AGAINST ALL WAR

HAVE NO FEAR OF PERFECTION. YOU'LL NEVER REACH IT.

NEW YORK CITY

New York City is one of the most vibrating and intense megapolis in the world where more than 80 languages are spoken at once. A city of extremes, it can bring out the best and the worst we all have inside and it can surely be defined in as many ways as citizens it holds.

www.santamonicabcn.com

All rights reserved. Artwork © 2010
Mark Brooks Graphik Design.
Santamonica LW.

SantaMonica
LegitimateWear

Design Institute of Australia Top 6 Design Icons

Buro North was engaged by the Design Institute of Australia (DIA) to develop an identity and suite of graphic material for their annual speaker series (Top 10×10) now in its 5th year. The Top 10x10 series is a fast paced, informative, showroom-based forum that attracts over 200 professional designers each year. Top 6×6 was held at Space Furniture's spectacular showroom in Richmond, facilitating both the social and educational aspects of the event. The theme for Top 6×6 was 'Design Icons'. Six of Australia's leading designers presented a personal selection of six of their favourite designs and the reasons for their choice. They could be environments, objects, graphics or experiences.

Taking the number 6 as a starting point for the design, Buro North developed the logotype based on a 6×6 grid, with intersecting lines creating the shapes of the letterforms. The shapes have been separated onto 6 different coloured paper stocks, and lasercut to produce the layered image, creating a depth of graphic that is relevant to the audience of interior designers and architects.

Team: Soren Luckins, Dave Williamson, Tim Dow
Photography: Shane Loorham

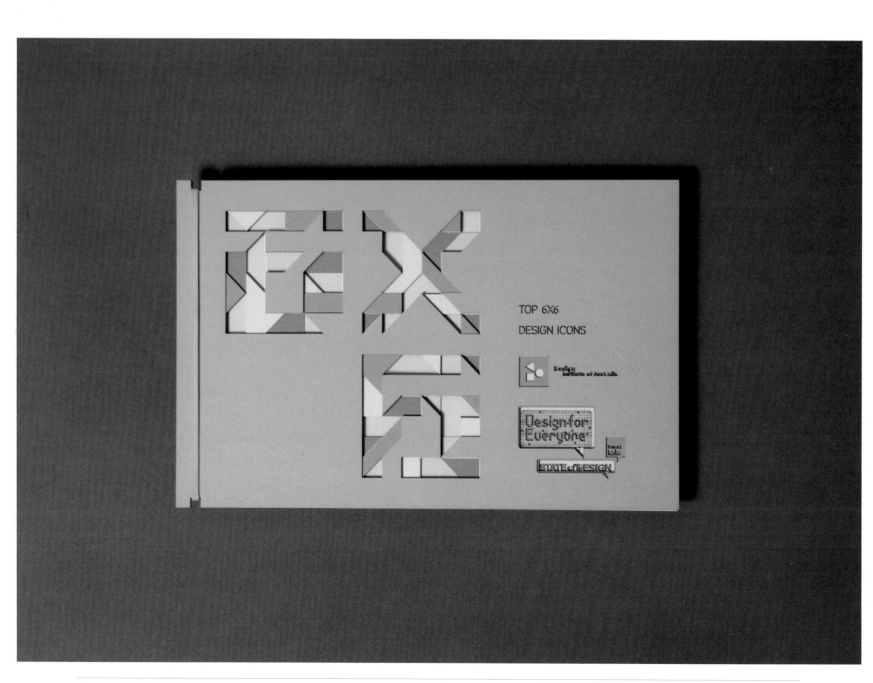

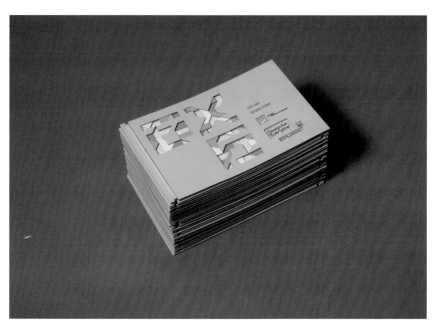

Buro North

Lightcycle

As part of the 2009 State of Design Festival Buro North developed the brand and collateral for the LightCycle competition.

Using 1 meter of LED strip lights and their imagination, participants were given the task of creating a light fixture to represent environmental sustainability.

A typographic solution for the brand was based on an LED inspired grid system, referencing the theme of the competition "Sampling the Future", then applied to promotional posters that were screenprinted by hand in black over a flouro blend.

Team: Soren Luckins, Sarah Napier, Shane Loorham
Photography: Shane Loorham

Chen Design Associates

Reel Centric

Brand and identity development for an online
video marketing company.

Creative Director: Joshua C. Chen
Brand Strategy: Margaret Hartwell
Art Directors: Joshua C. Chen, Laurie Carrigan
Designer: Jure Gavran

Chris Clarke

Gravesend — The death of community

Gravesend training centre is a small mock town situated in the borough of Gravesham, in Kent, England. Built by the Metropolitan Police in 2002 as a facsimile of an urban area, the 9,250 square meter development, constructed to meet the training requirements of the police, has all the appearance of being inhabited, except for the absence of any actual inhabitants. This surreal installation serves as a chilling account of the death of community in 21st century Britain.

While the global village expands, local collective identity and communication have dwindled, to the detriment of communal interest. We have estates, parks, nightclubs, tube stations, but is the community that is so starkly absent from Gravesend significantly more present in our inhabited cities and towns? Gravesend can be interpreted as a warning – a prophecy of society's potential to alienate itself from itself and kill its collective identity.

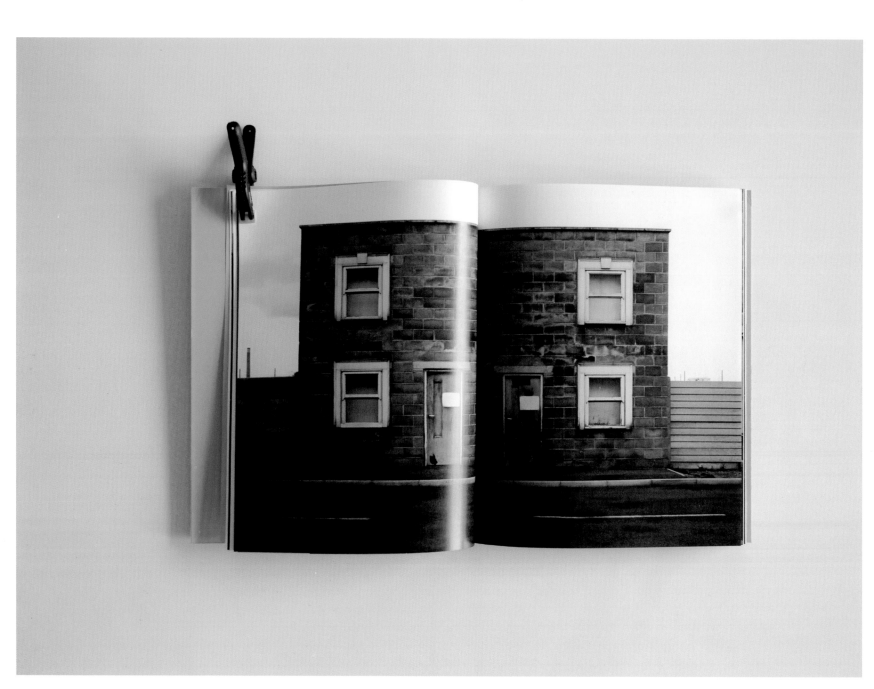

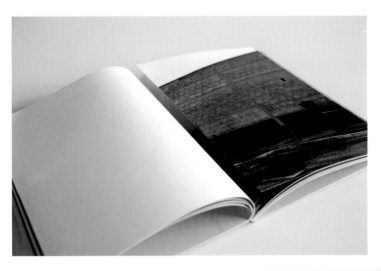

Good Typeface is Invisible

A typographical submission for the Ridiculous Typography Rules book. The rule that needed to be visualised was A Good Typeface is Invisible. The idea for this came from the question, when does text becomes an image (legible)? When we read text we don't see the alphabetical characters as images or icons, we interpret them collectvely as text. The result is an image out of which the word slowly appears, becoming... This submission was also used as a poster, in the typographic festival and exhibition Don't Believe The Type in The Hague.

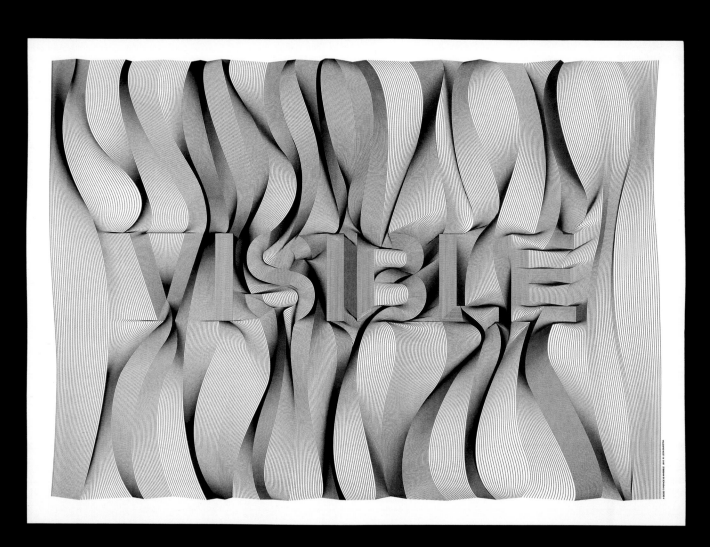

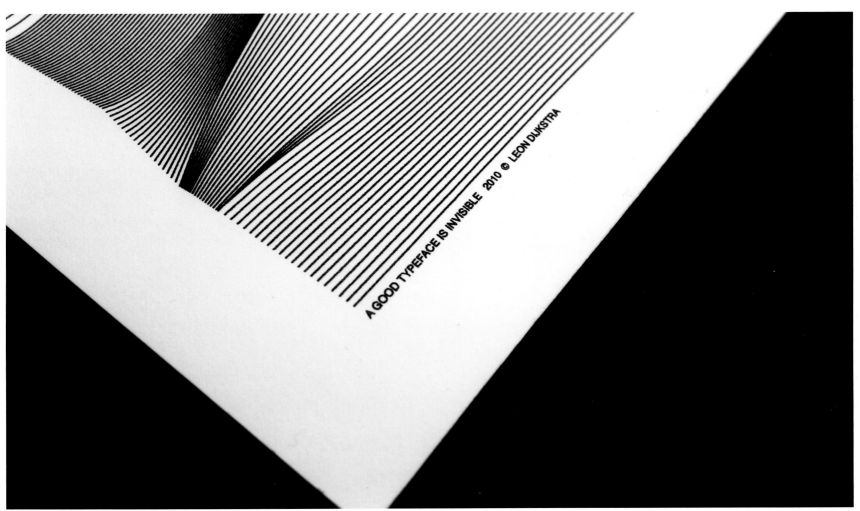

A GOOD TYPEFACE IS INVISIBLE 2010 © LEON DIJKSTRA

COOEE

Taking your pulse by webcam Illustration

For the 10th consecutive December issue, the
New York Times Magazine chose to look back
on the past year through a distinctive prism:
ideas. COOEE was asked to make an illustration
for the article: Taking Your Pulse by Webcam.

Joshua Distler

By: AMT

Logo, packaging and original typeface concept for designer Alissia Melka-Teichroew whose work decontextualizes items of value. The packaging aims to emphasize this by framing each product with a digitally rendered image of classical art.

Realized in cooperation with Mike Abbink

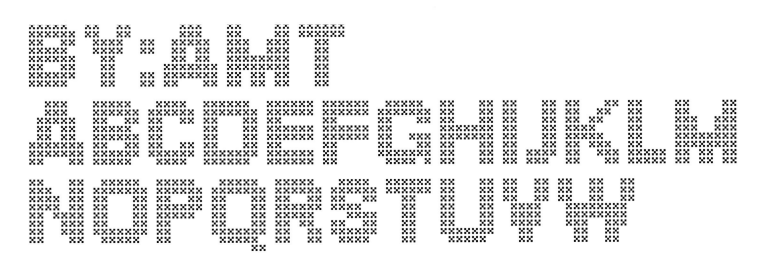

Doris & Associates Architects

Doris & Associates Architects provide a range of architectural services, from studies to building design. The brochure had to present in detail the different areas that the practice was working in, so it was divided into the following chapters: offices, commercial buildings, exhibition events and private home theatres.

The client wanted the graphic style to be both innovative and elegant and to express their architectural inspirations as well as the construction quality.

The brochure is in 3 languages (greek, english and german).

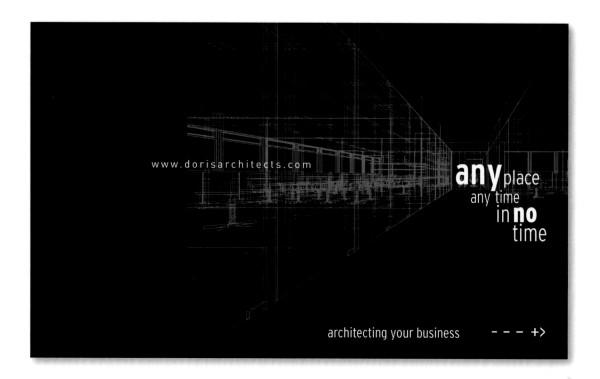

Βασ. Κωνσταντίνου 30, 11635 Αθήνα_**T** 210 7212000_**F** 210 7259546_**e** info@dorisarchitects.com www.dorisarchitects.com

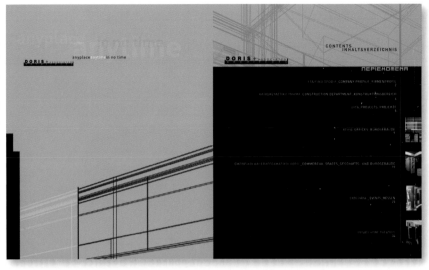

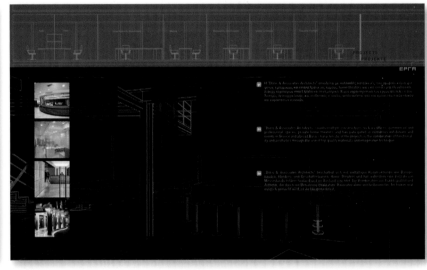

Photowall

During 2010 Dalston Creative worked on the Photowall brand. They had been asked to look at all their communication, identify the core brand values and unify the brand. In the end the designers decided to keep a large part of the well established brand unchanged but redrew the logo, added new colours and proposed new possibilities for expanding the company.

Everything was well documented in the 56 page brandguide they produced for the Photowall designers, third parties and employees to use. Everything from logotype size and positioning to colours, stationery etc. was defined and carefully documented. Dalston Creative's objective was to make the Photowall brand sleeker and stronger and widen its market appeal.

The brandguide was produced in wallpaper format as a brand launcher! It is currently in place at Photowall's office.

Dalston Creative also produced everything from instore advertising, information packs for wallpapers and product catalogues to canvas prints and a full redesign of the Photowall website.

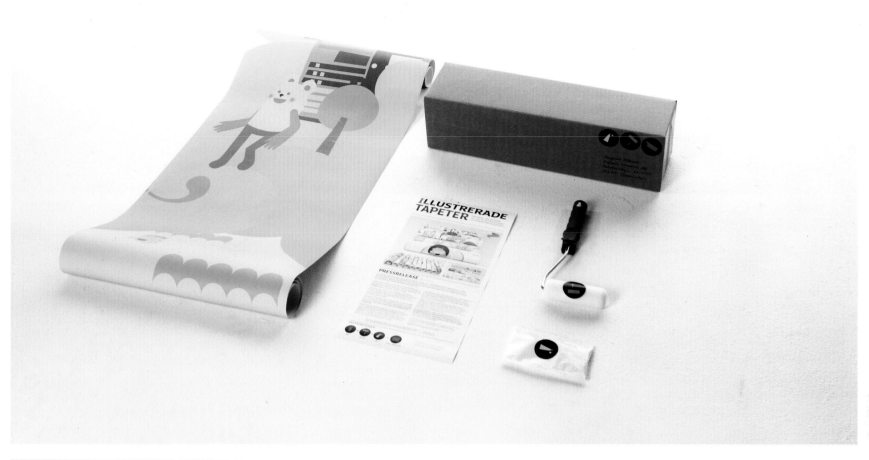

Biorhythm

This Science Gallery flagship exhibition explores the scientific and psychological connections between music and the body. Detail worked closely with the Science Gallery team on the promotional design including a broadsheet exhibition catalogue and exhibition graphics. The key image is the work of X-ray photographer Nick Veasey.

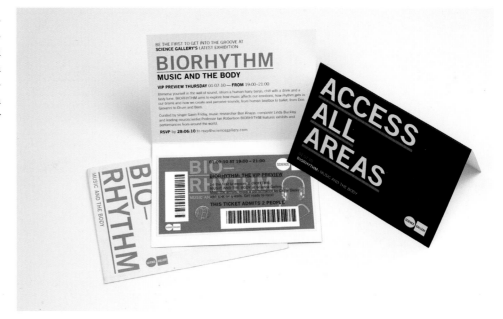

Detail

Love Lab

Love Lab at the Science Gallery was an exhibition which invited the public to take part in a series of research experiments from a number of different disciplines including neuroscience, psychology, genetics, physiology and biochemistry... all to help reveal the science behind our desires. Detail lovingly designed the promotional communications and exhibition graphics.

11:02:10–12:03:10
LOVE LAB
THE SCIENCE OF DESIRE
DO YOU DARE PUT YOURSELF TO THE TEST?

FEBRUARY 11–MARCH 12, 2010 TUES–FRI 12:00–20:00 & SAT–SUN 12:00–18:00
ADMISSION FREE [SUGGESTED DONATION €5]. FIND OUT MORE AT **WWW.SCIENCEGALLERY.COM**
SCIENCE GALLERY, PEARSE STREET, TRINITY COLLEGE, DUBLIN 2. T: +353 (0)1 896 4091

✿ Ulster Bank   **wellcome**trust   SCIENCE GALLERY IS AN INITIATIVE OF TRINITY COLLEGE DUBLIN

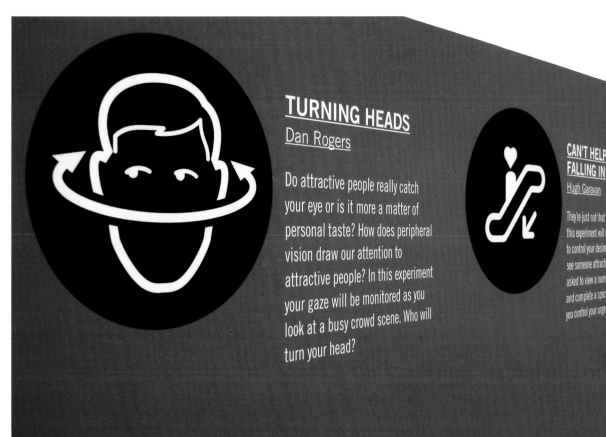

TURNING HEADS
Dan Rogers

Do attractive people really catch your eye or is it more a matter of personal taste? How does peripheral vision draw our attention to attractive people? In this experiment your gaze will be monitored as you look at a busy crowd scene. Who will turn your head?

CAN'T HELP FALLING IN LOVE
Hugh Garavan

They're just not that right for you – this experiment will test your ability to control your desires when you see someone attractive; you will be asked to view a number of faces and complete a specific task – can you control your urges?

AGELESS LOVE
Amrai Kaa Sethi

Do older and younger people perceive attractiveness differently and if so, how? This experiment allows you to view and hear unfamiliar faces and voices of all ages, then rate how you like them.

" **GRAVITATION IS NOT RESPONSIBLE FOR PEOPLE FALLING IN LOVE.** "

ALBERT EINSTEIN

Shift

Business concept, business management, web site design and architecture, packaging and identity for Shift, a font foundry.

Elixir Design

Buck & Rose Road Trip Productions

Lucasfilm needed an invitation to set the stage and expectations for a sneak preview of their new Letterman Digital Arts Center in The Presidio of San Francisco. The picnic gala, co-hosted by George Lucas, Francis Ford Coppola, Steve Jobs, and Saul Zaentz, would feature a dazzling array of local entertainers, from Joan Baez and Boz Scaggs to Michael Tilson Thomas (conductor of the San Francisco Symphony). Gourmet picnic baskets would showcase the artistry of renowned Bay Area chefs and specialty food producers.

Designers: Aine Coughlan, Nathan Durrant
Creative Director: Jennifer Jerde

Elixir helped this 25-year-old company reinvent itself verbally and visually. The Jerde Partnership had basically pioneered "experiential architecture" and the notion of "place-making," but was struggling with flat sales, low morale and a murky message. Elixir developed a branding strategy that clarified the brand accessibility and quantified the tremendous success of their projects. Elixir's research provided the basis for their subsequent redesign of all of The Jerde Partnership's visual communications.

Designers: Nathan Durrant, Aaron Cruse
Creative Director: Jennifer Jerde
Illustrator: Polly Becker
Writer: Rich Binell

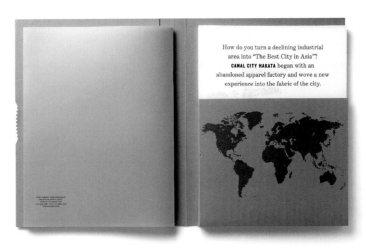

The Printing Bike

It's not often that one has the opportunity to be both the client and designer in a project. This degree project by Swedish design students Calle Enström and Johan Undén consisted of four bikes that had been assembled to create a four-colour press; a mechanical monster that was supposed to inspire while demonstrating the basic principles of a printing press. When the students came up wtih the idea they were struck with the thought that this was something they would regret not doing if they didn't see it through, and a month later they were glad to have gone with that gut feeling.

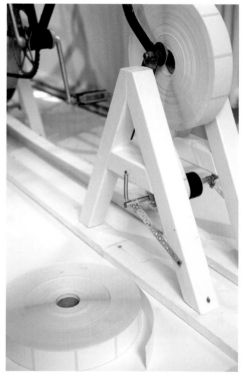

Evenson Design Group

Evenson Design Group

Evenson Design Group's (EDG) brand identity is simple, clean, and distinctive. This elegant logo is displayed on EDG's complete stationery suite, including their website.

Designers: Dallas Duncan, Tim Moraitis
Art Directors: Stan Evenson, Mark Sojka

4Lines' mission is to provide a platform for examining the work of four fashion designers with highly conceptual approaches, and to situate the interraction between art and design within the discourse of contemporary culture. Comprised of visionary fashion designers Nick Cave, Shane Gabier, Anke Loh, and Katrin Schnabl, 4Lines is a partnership that extends beyond the traditional definition of fashion. Faust provided concept, design, production, and print management relating to their identity and an opening event invitation.

Testimonials

This self-promotional piece by the graphic design studio, Faust, grew out of an idea from "the business side" of the partnership: "We gotta get serious and put something more business-y out there. Maybe we should assemble all of our great client testimonials into one piece." The creative team was underwhelmed by the idea; the project languished. Until, that is, the business side and the creative side were in the car discussing the project saying, "Maybe it would be funny to throw a testimonial in from someone who has no relevance to our business … like my mom … and our dry cleaner … and your waxing esthetician." Genius!

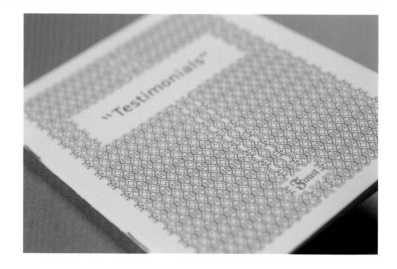

"I save all of Bobby's paintings—
I mean, you just never know if they'll
be worth something someday.
I never thought he could make a
living doing his art, but God bless."

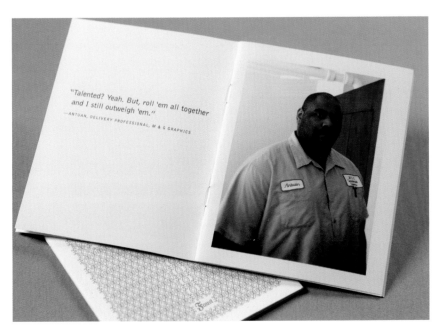

"Talented? Yeah. But, roll 'em all together and I still outweigh 'em."
—ANTUAN, DELIVERY PROFESSIONAL, M & G GRAPHICS

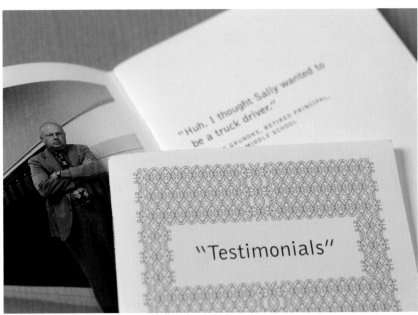

"Huh. I thought Sally wanted to be a truck driver."
— GRUNDKE, RETIRED PRINCIPAL, MIDDLE SCHOOL

"Testimonials"

"Testimonials"

"Baba gorp eeeeee p..."
LUCIA FAUST, DAUGHTER

" Though I've only known them a short while, Faust is able to solve

Focus24

Focus24 are a hire facility created by film-makers for filmmakers, exising to not only provide cutting edge production equipment but also deliver supporting services to film and television shoots.

The brief provided to Fridge Creative required a strong, bold identity which could be used consistently across a wide range of media.

It was applied to stationery, stickers, equipment labels, door signs, vans, their website, emailers and much more.

FOCUS 24
JUST ADD ACTION!

+44 (0) 20 7033 6555
www.focus24.tv
info@focus24.tv

30 HOXTON SQUARE
SHOREDITCH
LONDON
N1 6NN

15 BATEMAN STREET
SOHO
LONDON
W1D 3AQ

Angel De Armas

Angel De Armas loves film and creates cinematic quality wedding films from Seattle, Washington and Honolulu, Hawaii. The custom dvd package and business card are printed offset litho with gloss black foil stamping. The dvd is silkscreened gloss black on matte black.

SEA / HNL

MY LOVE FOR FILM...

...when I was very young. Our family had just left Cuba. Castro had taken over the co...
...many changes were taking place in the world, not just in politics, but also in fa...
...e eventually moved to Mexico City, where we lived just a few blocks away fr...
...Usually, late at night, I would sneak out of the house and walk to the thu...
...to some of the most creative and innovative directors of our time — ...
...me a few. They all had a grasp on me and I kept my eye on all of th...
...inated by the weird and wonderful way that only Fellini and Ru...
...uld hold a static shot for so long, or Kubrick could ta...
..., there could be a thousand explanations fo...
...ime to grow up and I wou...
...that chang...

ANGEL DE ARMAS
productions

Films by Francesco

Engraving, silk-screen, letterpress and offset combine to create stationery and packaging as beautiful and unique an experience as the client's films.

Stillmotion Photo + Film

Stillmotion is an internationally recognized wedding photo and film studio that creates artful images and provides industry education. The business card is letterpress printed in metallic silver with the mark die-cut.

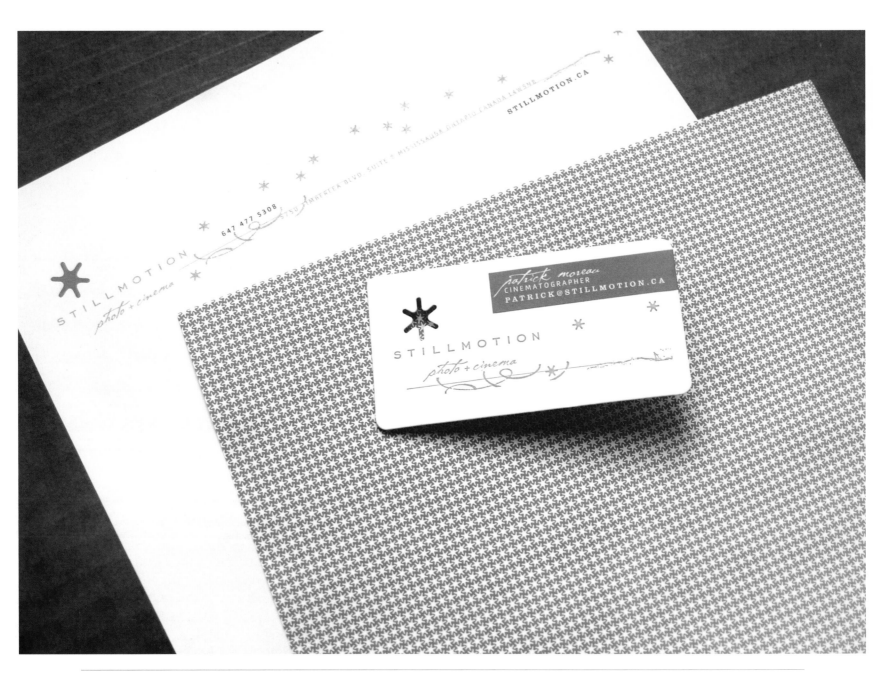

gdloft

Volume No. 1: Form vs. Function AIGA Lecture Series

This piece was created to advertise the Spring 2007 lecture series for AIGA Philadelphia. The series gathers together a group of designers that challenge traditional notions of graphic design. The goal was to create a piece that would both resonate with designers and stay true to the objectives of the lecture series. The poster intends to challenge the viewer by having him or her question the design of the poster and the completeness of the design, issues akin to the topics of lecture series itself.

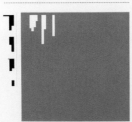

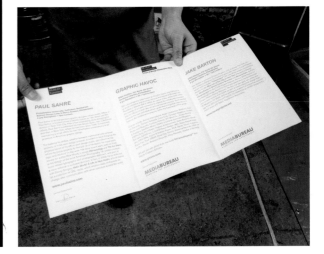

Philadelphia Design Awards, Call for Entries Mailer

In order to promote the design community, the AIGA Philadelphia developed their first regional design competition (PDA). gdloft was asked to conceptualize, design and overlook the copywriting of the sixteen page call for entries brochure. gdloft developed the concept "Show some love" to play off the acronym "PDA". The concept revolves around the idea that "PDA" (Philadelphia Design Awards) can help build a sense community among designers as well as becoming a motivating impetus (love) to creating good design work.

The text is playfully made up of the top ten motivating phrases. In addition, as a metaphor for building community, the brochure can be desconstructed, and pieced together to reveal a poster.

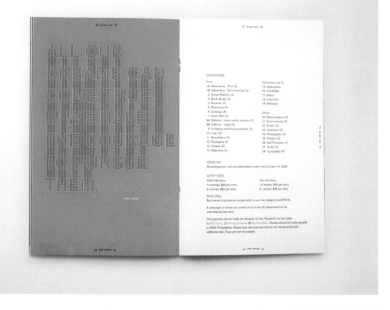

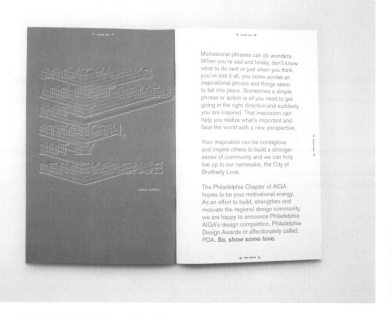

gdloft

Philadelphia Design Awards Catalogue

The project is a catalogue design for the American Institute of Graphic Arts, Philadelphia Design Competition. In the preliminary stages of the catalogue, gdloft focused on representing all designs, winners or not, as well as creating a book to serve as "art" within the context of a gallery (for the winners' exhibition). The catalogue print-run was limited to the number of entries received to represent all the work of the design community. Using a variable printing program, each cover is a different colour from a predetermined spectrum; thus, making each catalogue entirely unique— no two pieces are identical. In addition, each catalogue was individually numbered. When all the catalogues are stacked together the spines create a seamless spectrum of colour that has the quality of a sculpture.

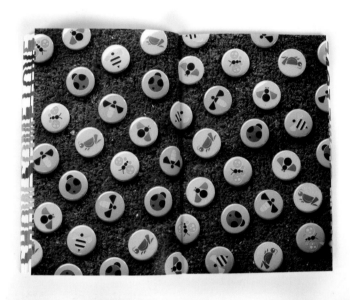

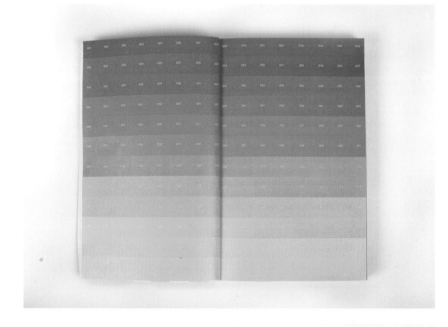

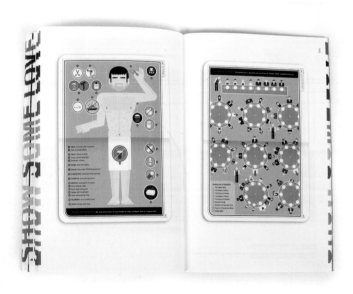

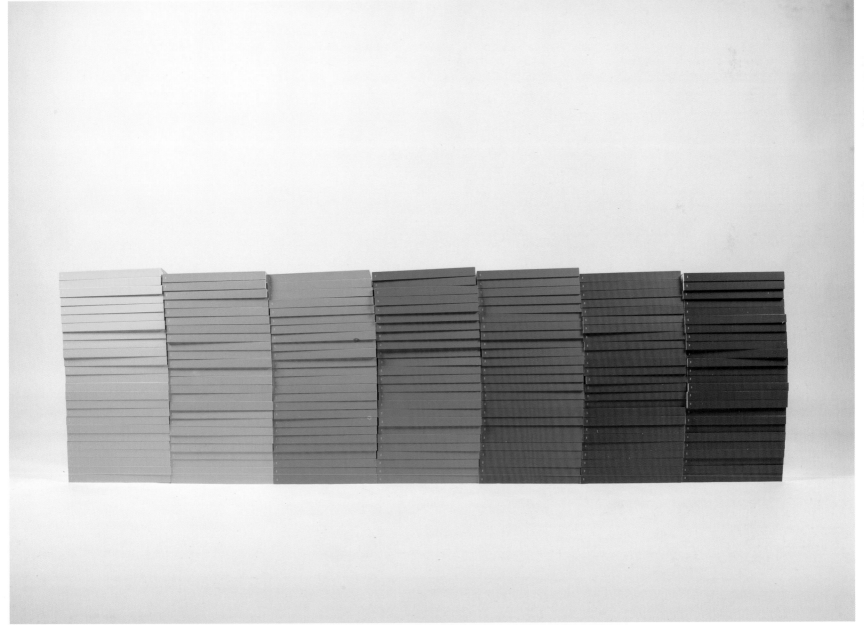

Imitation - Interpretation - Transformation - Metamorphosis

Thesis by Doris Freigofas about illustrations of fairy tales by the Brothers Grimm.

Designer: Doris Freigofas, Daniel Dolz
Client: School of Art Berlin Weißensee

Anna Härlin

Anna Härlin printed her business and greeting cards with a Gocco printer. Gocco is a Japanese color screenprinting system developed in 1977 by Noboru Hayama. Unfortunately these clever little machines are no longer produced today. Härlin was lucky enough to buy one and used it to print her series of cards. She printed a small edition of 100 pieces with 3 colours.

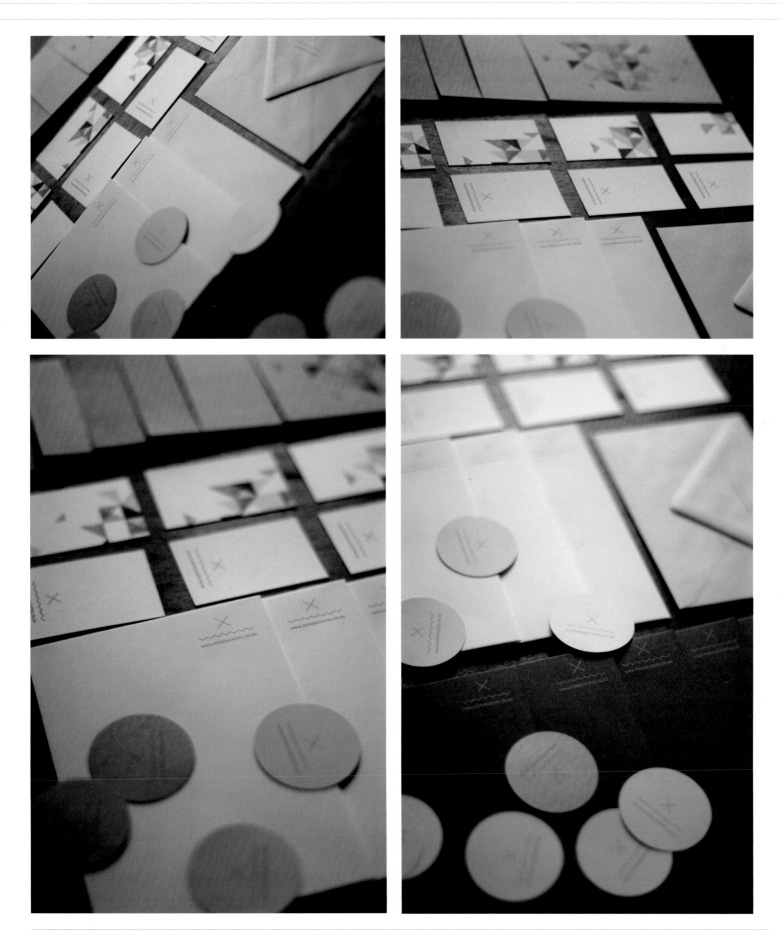

Anna Härlin

Britzka Film

Britzka Film focusses on direction and procuction of documentary films. Anna Härlin developed the new logo and corporate design for Britzka Film. The holiday cards were hand printed with a silk screen printer in an edition of 300 cards.

Self-Promotion 2009

Self-promotion is an important tool at post-graduate shows. For this particular occasion Alberto Hernández designed some special business cards. These could be unfolded allowing people to see an image and torn apart along perforated lines in order to separate off the little cards with the contact details.

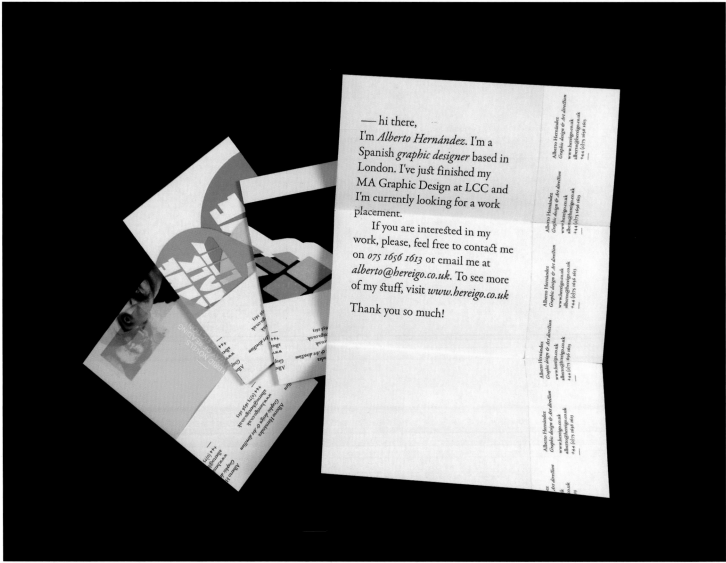

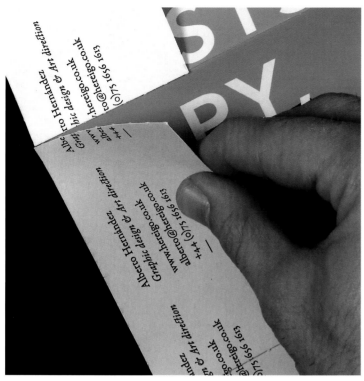

Mailers 2010

Printed literature is one of the primary tools of promotion for a designer. After finishing his studies, Alberto Hernández decided to design some mailers to promote his work by either posting them to studios or leaving them behind after interviews. Each mailer contains a résumé and 5 different projects.

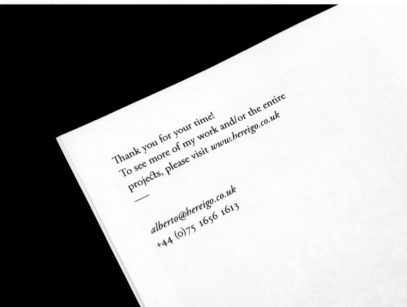

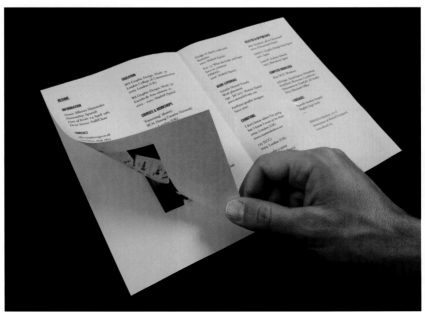

Design your Own Show

Held at the Madrid-Barajas International Airport in 2007, 'Diez por diez' was an exhibition that celebrated the centenary of Escuela de Arte número 10, featuring the work of its alumni.

To aid the task of designing an exhibition in such a complex space, a 'catalogue of elements' was produced. This included a group of 2D and 3D objects (such as street banners, foam letters and mobiles), which could be used to articulate the exhibition space and permitted the development of a flexible and modular system for the content. As the exhibition was designed to travel to different locations, the catalogue system made it possible to choose from among the elements to resolve each exhibition space.

In collaboration with Ana Laura Rojas.

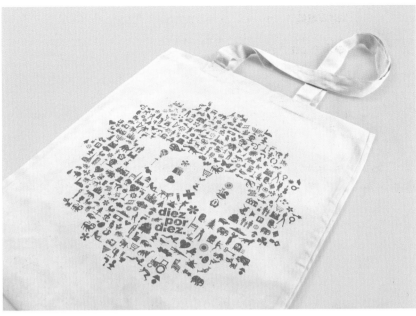

Design vs Music

Design vs Music is an event held alongside the annual Insomnia festival in Tromsø, Norway. In 2009 Heydays was hired by Scott Hansen of ISO50 to design publicity material for the event. They designed a 70 × 100 cm poster. It is undoubtedly influenced by Gottlieb Soland and Josef Müller-Brockmann's music posters. Instead of using the gramaphone image, they decided to base the poster on the white label sleeve, such as typically accompanied 90's hip-hop records. By die cutting a hole, the poster resembles a sleeve. But it also highlights details from posters underneath it, most of them music related. This gives room for reflecting on the topic "design vs music". Print finish includes die cut (12 inch circle) and silver Pantone on 150g matte paper.

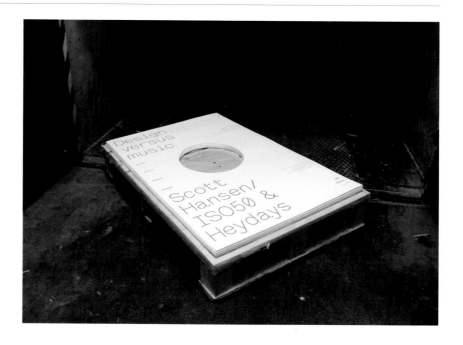

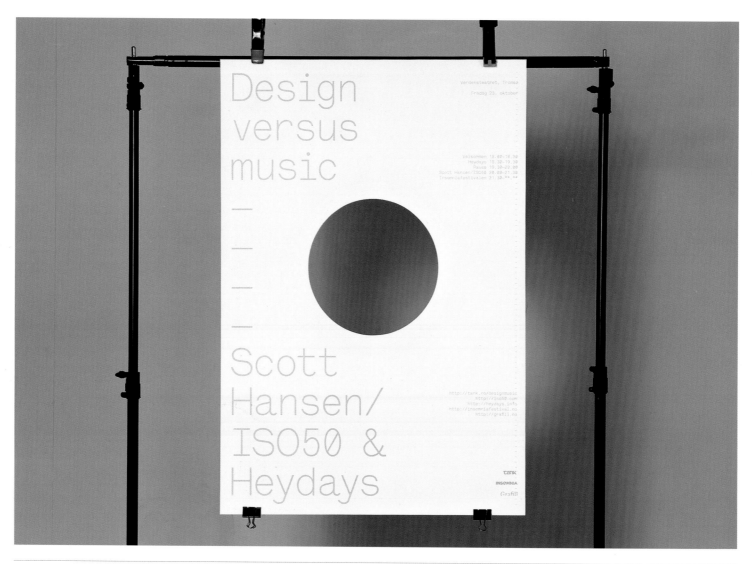

Heydays

Heydays' own stationery. Only one typeface is used in limited sizes. The shiny chrome is used as a reference to their name. The use of cardboard contrasts with this, it is for more functional, everyday use. The functionality of the elements is further reinforced with the extensive use of customized tape. Print finishing includes blind emboss, mirrorboard, cardboard and silkscreened jewelcases.

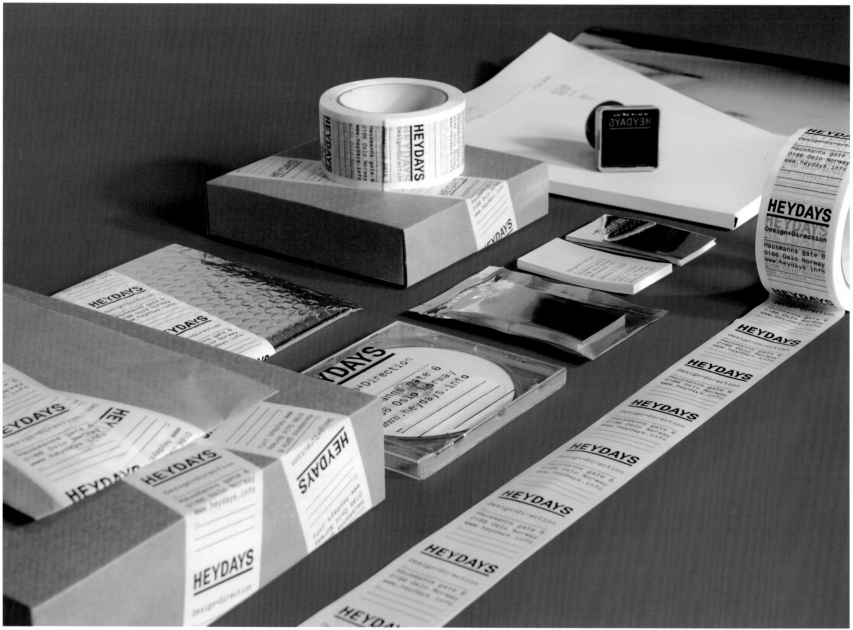

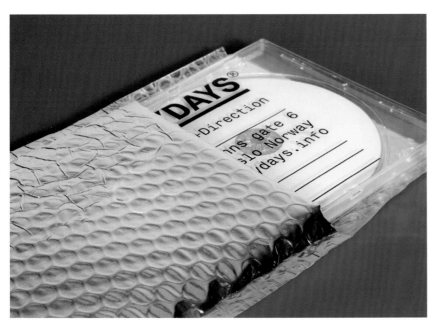

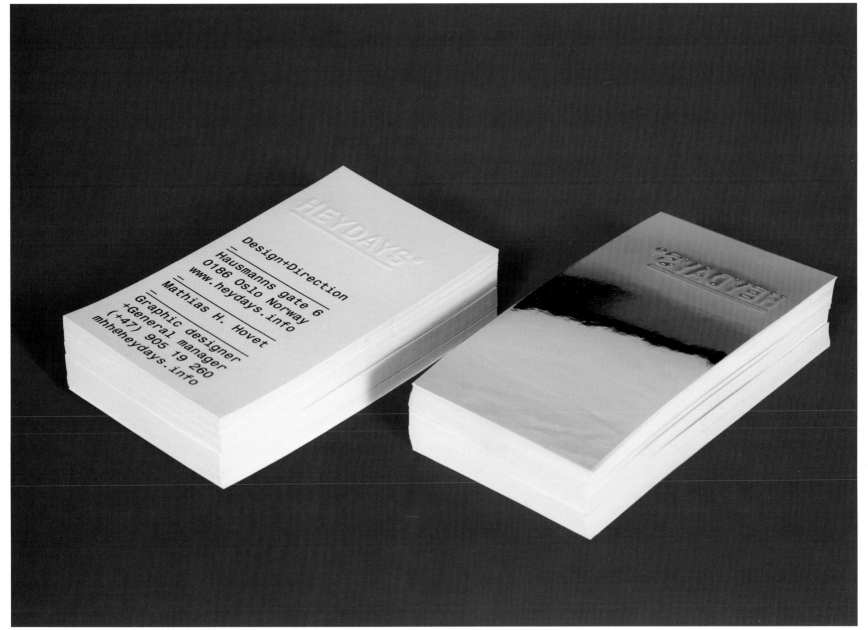

Frøystad+Klock

A small identity for furniture designers Frøystad+Klock, inspired by Scandinavian design traditions and their clever use of materials. A stripped down minimalist approach is ensured by focusing on details in the wordmark like the plus, Ã~ and O, and the way they stand together. Twelve photos of different materials were combined with coloured papers to differentiate the cards of the two designers. This also allows flexibility, as each element can be shown a number of ways within the same strict setup.

FRØYSTAD +KLOCK

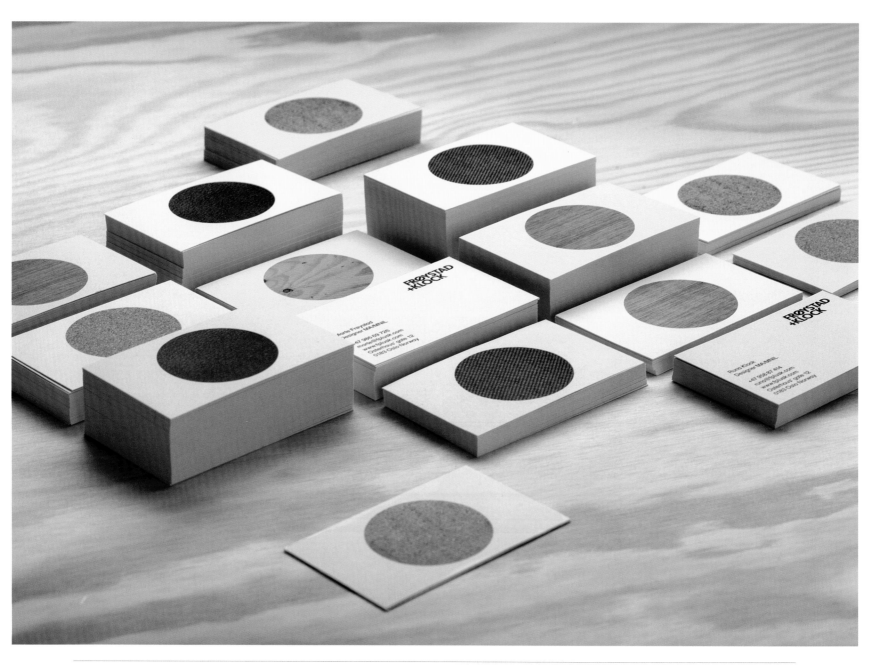

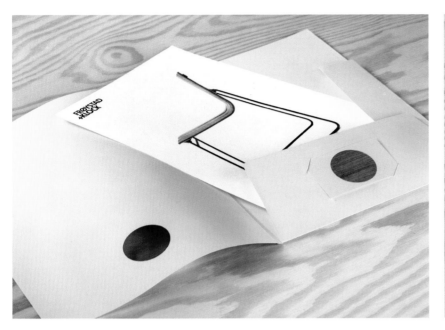

Grip: kultur

Grip: kultur is a company that holds cultural and creative workshops to give new spark to and refresh the outlook of businesses. Heydays was responsible for both the naming of the company and their visual identity. The logo is based on the idea of change, a movement from one place to another. All printed matter has been spot varnished to simulate the feel of paint (one of their workshops is in art), while it also is a reference to the word Norwegian word 'grip'.

Grip:

Daniel Acker

Logo and business card for photographer
Daniel Acker.

Use My Mind is a publicity company based in Sydney, Australia. James Kape was commissioned to create an entire update of both their logo design and associated identity. When designing the logo, he decided to shorten the name 'Use My Mind' to its acronym 'umm..' to create a more thought provoking representation and in doing so, it became representative of a public relations 'speak'. This was so well recieved that they later changed their name to 'umm..'

Oliver James Gosling

Oliver Gosling, a new breed of web developer based in Bristol, UK needed a brand identity that demonstrated his aim of providing top class technical skills with a very personal, 'human friendly' service.

Hype & Slippers developed an identity heavily influenced by information graphics and implemented this style into an online portfolio (www.goslingo.com), CV mailer and stationery. The clean, technical feel of these materials was contrasted with several humorous touches including comparing his height to that of an elephant, and references to his daily average intake of tea!

OLIVER JAMES GOSLING WEB DEVELOPER

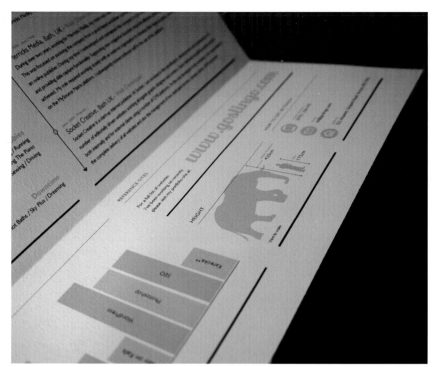

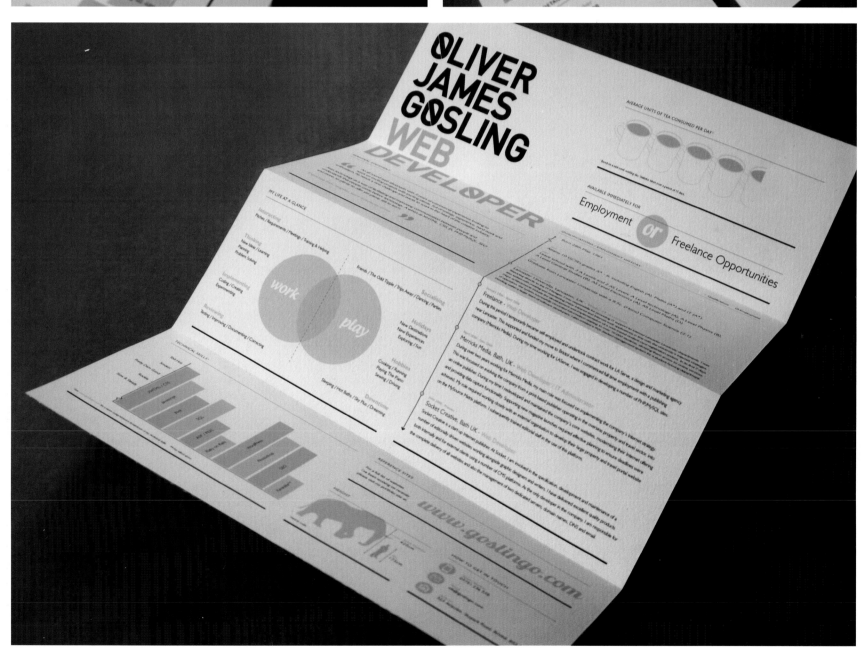

The Commons Brooklyn

The Commons Brooklyn is a place to learn, work, play, and share. Its mission is to protect the forms of wealth that are not owned by private entities: those that belong to all of us. These include but are not limited to: fresh water, wilderness, the oceans, public institutions, language, culture, the internet, open source communities, volunteer networks, and more.

Melissa Ennen, the founder of The Commons, asked Hyperakt to develop a flexible identity system that could adapt itself to the broad range of community-based issues her organization is involved in.

Creative Direction & Design: Julia Vakser, Deroy Peraza
Design: Jason Lynch

cdi magazine

cdi is a new publication from the Centro de la Imagen, in Mexico, that promotes photographic work from young students, well-known photographers and historical sources with a particular graphic design approach.

The graphic concept proposed by the designers at Ideo Comunicadores was for the layout of the publication to be fresh and responsive to the differeneces between the widely ranging photographic material included, which comprised colour photography by young photographers, classic archive photographs, historic images in contact format and images from photo albums, etc. In editorial pages cdi's logo was used to reinforce the identity of the magazine.

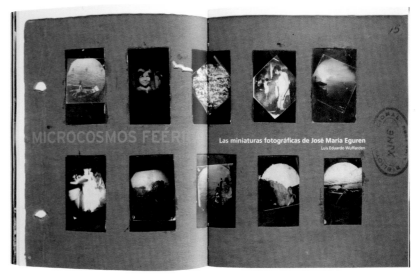

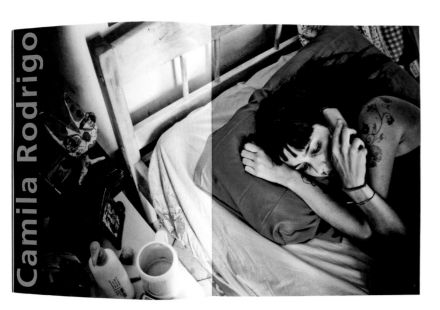

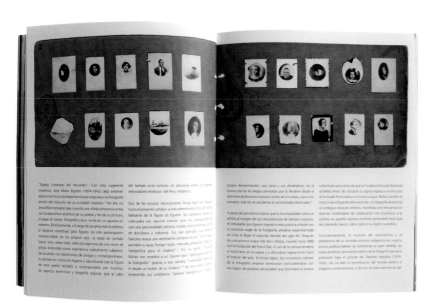

This is a book with a collection of the designer's work from the past two years as a form of
self-promotion. The book itself is made with
a brown box card cover coupled with yellow
buckram down the side. The inside pages were
printed digitally with a printer which uses
toner based inks.

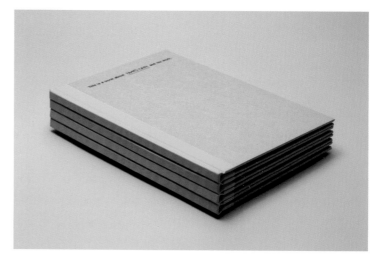

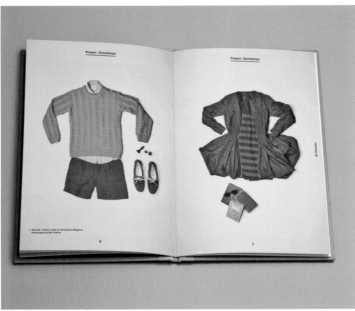

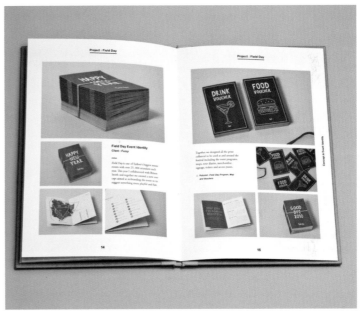

Schmuckmuseum Pforzheim

These posters are part of a comprehensive corporate design programme that also includes exhibition/museum design and signage. Based on a stringent typographical concept, a dialogue is generated in the posters between typography and image, between exhibit and its translation into typography.

L2M3 Kommunikationsdesign GmbH

Württembergischer Kunstverein Stuttgart

The open corporate image of the Kunstverein in Stuttgart is founded on few, if constant parameters. The designs themselves display a certain stance towards graphic design and its tasks in a sphere whose conditions are constantly being discussed anew – art. In this way the designers try to find a "translation" that fits the particular theme of each exhibition and that acts as a visual representation.

Die Chronologie der Teresa Burga
Berichte, Diagramme, Intervalle / 29.9.11
30. September 2011 – 8. Januar 2012
Württembergischer Kunstverein Stuttgart

Landschaft (Entfernung)
31. März – 10. Juni 2007
Württembergischer Kunstverein Stuttgart

Re-Designing the East
Politisches Design in Asien und Europa
25. September 2010 – 9. Januar 2011
Württembergischer Kunstverein Stuttgart

NOH Suntag
Ausnahmezustand / State of Emergency / 비상국가
1. März – 18. Mai 2008
Württembergischer Kunstverein Stuttgart

19.01. – 26.02.2006
württembergischer kunstverein stuttgart
expanded media. medien im raum
wettbewerb des 19. stuttgarter filmwinters + malcolm le grice

Eine Tagung der Akademie Schloss Solitude,
des Hospitalhofs Stuttgart und des
Württembergischen Kunstvereins Stuttgart

Zensur in der Kunst?
Neue Mechanismen und Strategien
5. und 6. Dezember 2008
Württembergischen Kunstvereins Stuttgart

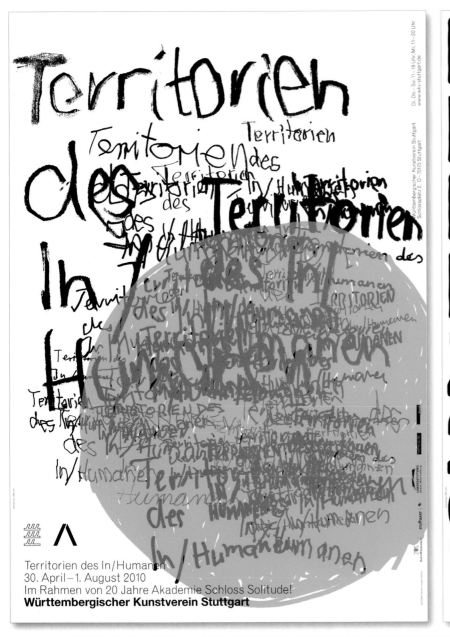

Territorien des In/Humanen
30. April – 1. August 2010
Im Rahmen von 20 Jahre Akademie Schloss Solitude!
Württembergischer Kunstverein Stuttgart

DIE KUNST, NICHT DERMASSEN REGIERT ZU WERDEN. 28.11.2010 – 9.1.2011

Die Kunst, nicht dermaßen regiert zu werden
28. November 2010 – 9. Januar 2011
Württembergischer Kunstverein Stuttgart

Dansmakers

Dansmakers (formerly known as Danswerkplaats Amsterdam) gives young choreographers room to perform, experiment and develop themselves. Lava made an identity in which dance and movement are translated into typography.

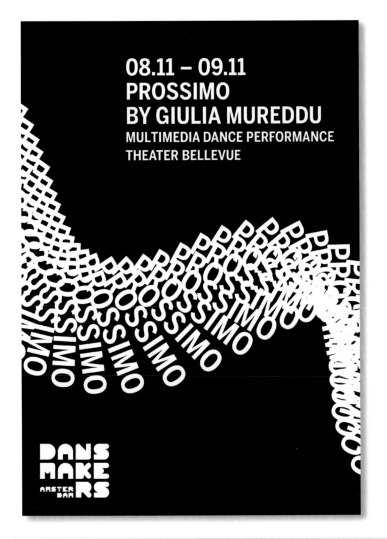

Interval Business Cards

Business cards for the two directors/creators of artist platform, Interval. Interval is an independent artist-led platform with a focus on new media practice.

Printed on 350gsm recycled uncoated stock. Gold metallic foil on the front, foiled varnish on the back. The designer was told that you can't do a Spot UV on an uncoated stock because it just soaks it up so he used a technique where you actually foil a varnish in the same way that you foil a colour. This enables the varnish to sit on the surface. Because it is done on uncoated stock there is a big contrast between the feel of the two elements - the rough, recycled stock and the smooth varnish. It allows the image to be really vibrant without the use of ink. The foil technique also gives you a subtle embossed effect on the images.

Flyers made out of lithographic plates. The image was exposed onto lithographic plates; these plates were then guillotined down to 1/3 A4 flyer size. The exposed image comes out silver on the plate. The image will start to fade in around 3 months' time...

Interval Postcards

Generic promotional item for Interval. Printed on 350gsm greyboard. Foiled with metallic cyan on the front and black gloss foil on the back. The cyan really takes off when the light hits it and provides an extreme colour contrast against the greyboard. It's also interesting to have something from a period textbook represented in an unorthodox way. Black is used to convey the information on the reverse. The designers wanted to use a grey and a really vibrant colour at the same time to generate an unusual mix of extremes. In terms of touch/texture, the greyboard has a nice rough feel to it that provides a nice contrast with the smooth metallic foil. The design also continues with the idea of not using any ink which was used in the business cards for the same organisation.

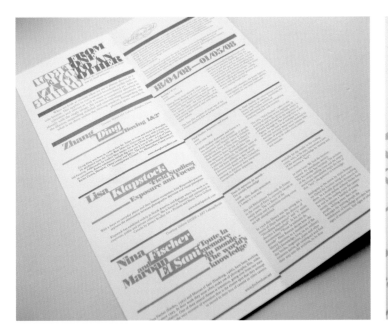

Turnstile

Turnstile was a rolling multimedia exhibition held over three days that featured a different set of artists each day. The designs were based on the idea of a turnstile tear-off ticket with a stub for each day of the exhibition. The bold numbers convey the central idea of three different days. In the folding posters a different strategy is used to distinguish the 3 different days.

Flyer — letterpressed in gold and perforated in 3 places on box board.

Folding posters — full colour digital on bible paper.

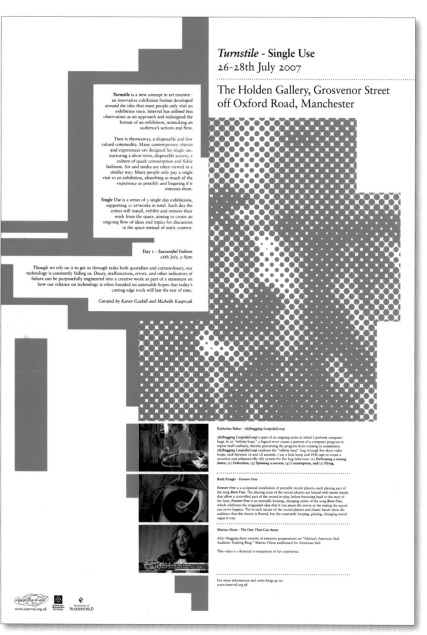

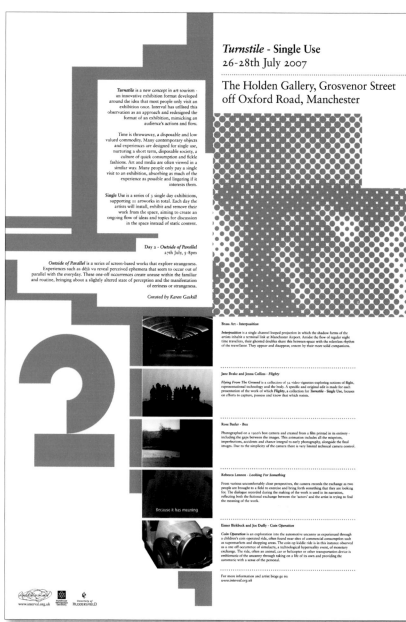

Turnstile - Single Use
26-28th July 2007

The Holden Gallery
Grosvenor Street
Off Oxford Road
Manchester

Turnstile is a new concept in art tourism - an innovative exhibition format developed around the idea that most people only visit an exhibition once. Interval utilizes this observation as an approach and has redesigned the production of an exhibition, mimicking an audience's actions and flow.

Single Use is a series of 3 single day exhibitions, supporting 11 artworks in total. Each day the artists will install, exhibit and remove their work from the space, aiming to create an ongoing flow of ideas and topics for discussion.

www.interval.org.uk

3

Day 3 - *Portable Rest*
28th July, 2-5pm

Is rest portable? Has it become a commodity that you can take to the park and experience? *Portable Rest* sees artworks that induce, create or represent relaxation, questioning how we can be proactive in being inactive. Audience members are asked to bring suitable accessories for relaxation; rugs, mats, picnics, etc.

2

Day 2 - *Outside of Parallel*
27th July, 5-8pm

Outside of Parallel is a series of screen-based works that explore strangeness. Experiences such as déjà vu reveal perceived ephemera that seem to occur out of parallel with the everyday. These one-off occurrences create unease within the familiar and routine, bringing about a slightly altered state of perception and the manifestation of eeriness or strangeness.

1

Day 1 - *Successful Failure*
26th July, 5-8pm

Though we rely on it to get us through tasks both quotidian and extraordinary, our technology is constantly failing us. Decay, malfunctions, errors, and other indicators of failure can be purposefully engineered into a creative work as part of a statement on how our reliance on technology is often founded on untenable hopes that today's cutting edge tools will last the test of time.

The Lab

Logo, CD release, promotional postcards, letterheads and gig posters for Manchester art & record label "The Lab".

The Lab's definition of itself is expressed in the following quotation: *"We're a label / agency - whatever you'd like to call us. Along with putting out records, we'll be hosting exciting events, 'release' very ltd clothing, art work, and maybe even curate an exhibition or two. And a whole lot more..."*

CD wallet is letterpressed in Metallic Silver, CD label is printed in Neon Pantone 805. Postcards and letterheads are printed in Pantone Green. Gig posters are limited to 100 copies and are printed in Neon Pantone 805 on an old litho press.

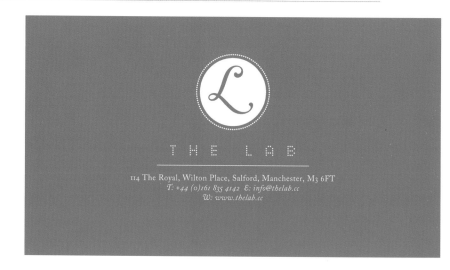

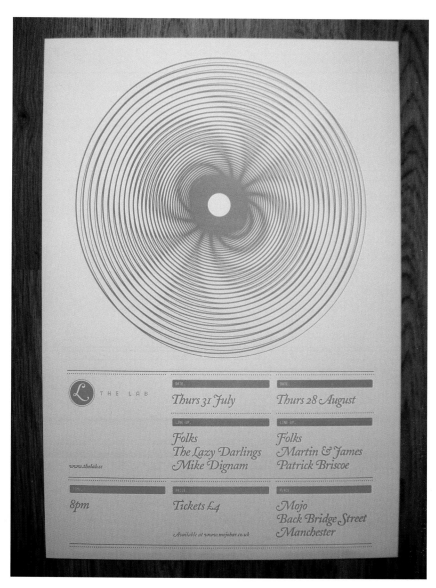

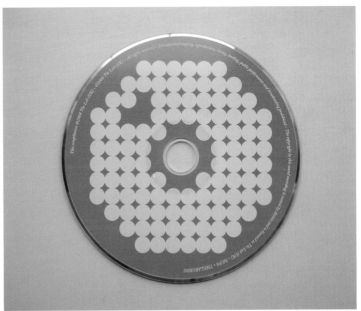

Creative Collective Effect

Creative Collective is a fashion show that is held during Stockholm Fashion Week. Lundgren+Lindqvist designed the identity for the show comprising a blog, a logotype, posters and flyers plus a set of stickers. The key words of the identity were recycling, collaboration, engagement and creativity. This was emphasized on the poster by cutting the logotype into six different pieces and mixing them up to create a graphical pattern. The paper was perforated so that the pieces could be ripped apart and fitted back together to form the logotype. This is a spur to people to use their creativity and symbolizes the acts of collaboration and recycling. The perforations were set to resemble stitches on garments.

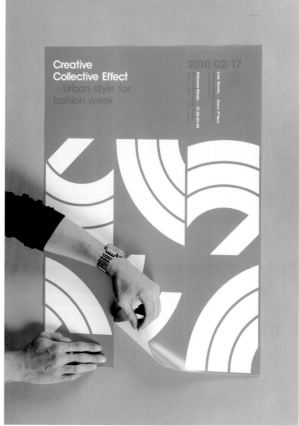

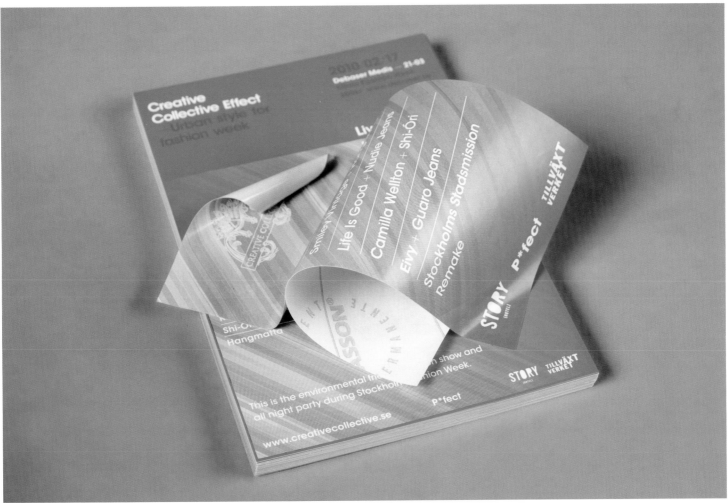

Jennie Smith Photo

Lundgren+Lindqvist have been working with talented photographer Jennie Smith for some time now and have previously designed her identity, website and business cards. Upon her return to Sweden from a year long trip to Sydney, Australia, they decided that it was time to update her business cards.

Working with a set of photos that Jennie Smith had taken of the roof of the Met Center in central Sydney, Lundgren+Lindqvist created three different business card backs. The images were cropped and printed in duo tone, with the turquoise used throughout the identity, to make them more of a graphical pattern than an actual image. The double N symbol used in the logotype was silver foiled on the back while the front of the card was kept clean and sober, to avoid an overly busy appearance in combination with the patterns on the backs of the cards.

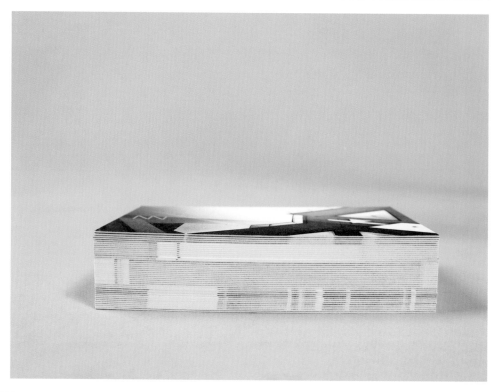

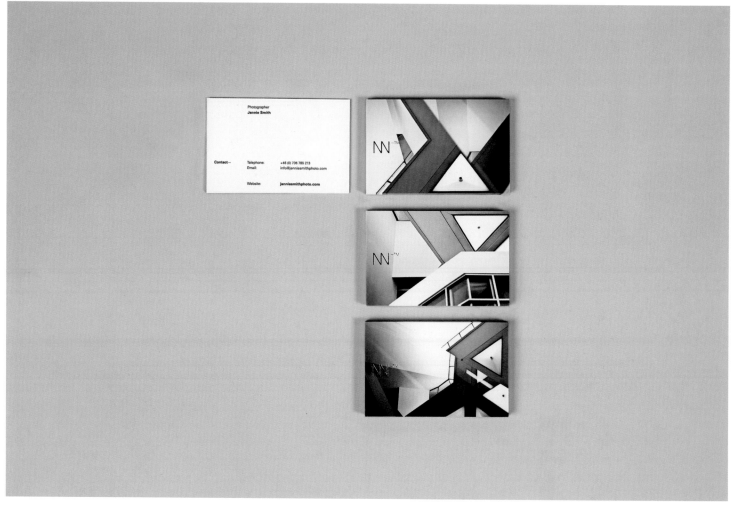

Philip Ljungström is a very talented photographer based in Gothenburg, Sweden. He works in several different fields including fashion and extreme sports.

Lundgren+Lindqvist designed Philip's business cards and collaborated on a promotional poster for Victor Västernäs, a top sailor aiming to compete in the London Olympics in 2012. The poster was printed on Arctic Paper's Munken Rough paper, a brand new stock that was not officially released at the time.

Johanna Lenander

Johanna Lenander is a writer and editor living and working in New York City. Johanna is also the author of the book Hair Wars. Working for prestigious clients, such as Style Magazine (New York Times), Elle, Gucci and Karl Lagerfeld, Johanna needed a site that not only displayed her writing skills but also reflected her sense of style. We were approached to design and build the site and to design Johanna Lenander's identity and printed matter.

The site was built so that it would give the visitor a quick overview enabling them to assess the information of interest rapidly. The aesthetic, both of the identity and website, follows the editorial tradition of classic newspapers, but with a modern twist. We used the WordPress CMS as a platform for the site which enables Johanna to easily edit the site and upload new work.

Printing techniques include relief and fluorescent inks, and high quality paper stock such as the uncoated Munken Polar 400gsm was used for the stationery.

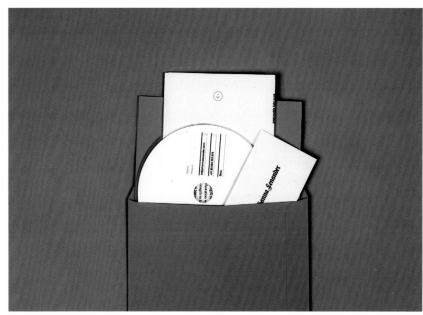

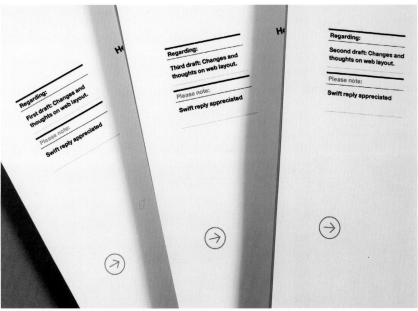

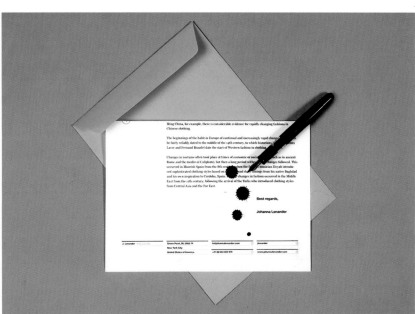

Lundgren+Lindqvist

In the autumn of 2009, the team at Lundgren+Lindqvist came to the realization that it was time for them to rethink their visual identity. They had travelled quite some way since first starting out and the old identity and website suddenly felt to them like a pair of old worn-out jeans.

Their new business cards are triplexed GF Smith Colorplan (Cool Grey, Bright Red and Pristine White) and have negative embossing, foil blocking and UV-varnish. The letter paper is Colorplan Pristine White with negative embossing and the S65 window envelopes are made out of Colorplan Cool Grey.

The promotional poster is printed on both sides on MultiArt Silk paper with partial UV-varnish and water-varnish finishing. One side displays a screenshot from the website and the other the underlying code, two sides of our business. The intentional typo in the headline (neue instead of new) hints at the use of the Helvetica Neue typeface throughout the identity.

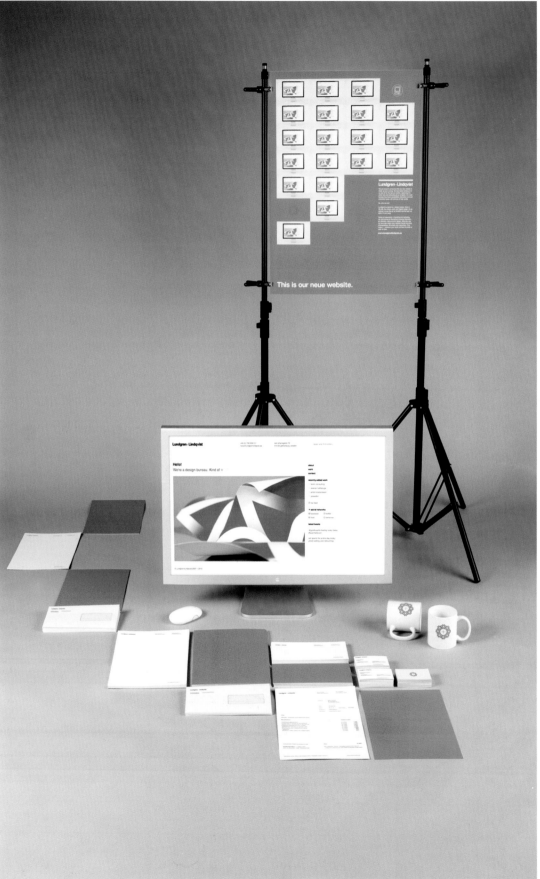

Lundgren+Lindqvist

The Healing Arts

The Healing Arts is a London based collective that "was born out of a desire to explore both the collective creative process, and an interest in how ideas propagate. It originally formed around an interest in experimental music but we quickly realized a shared curiosity for the arts, science, technology and society at large." Lundgren+Lindqvist were approached to design and develop The Healing Arts identity and web presence. After narrowing down the group's influences to a few key areas, such as mysticism, symbolism and alchemy, the designers began the process of developing the identity. While researching the themes, they stumbled upon Antahkarana, an ancient Tibetan symbol for healing. The meaning of Antahkarana in many ways related to the values of the collective while also incorporating the mysticism and symbolism. Hence, they used the symbol as the basis for the new logotype.

The letters of the word mark, that are based on the Replica typeface (Lineto), were interlaced to make the mark more compact and unique.

The foiled business cards were designed as the three separate parts of the symbol, each card carrying one of the initials on the back.

The Healing Arts members are all active on a number of networks and websites across the web and therefore our main idea for their website was to aggregate as much of that activity as possible in to the collective's site. Using the network's API's and RSS feeds we incorporated members' feeds from Facebook, Twitter, Flickr and Soundcloud into the site, as well as some of the members' personal blogs.

Lundgren+Lindqvist

A-Z Wedding Book

When a designer gets married there's a lot of pressure to design the entire experience - they're wired to craft something beautiful, personal and customized for the event. The A-Z book was no exception to this rule. It was designed to tell the stories of the bride and groom's major life events to that point.

A sophisticated yet minimal illustration approach was created to work with the factual copy style. The resulting piece was a small book containing twenty six vignettes that the wedding attendees could take home as a keepsake commemorating the event.

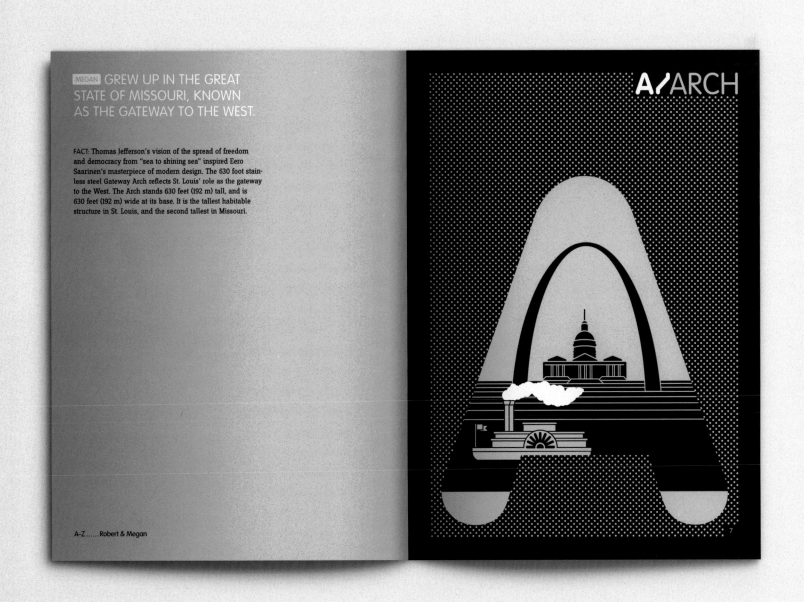

MEGAN GREW UP IN THE GREAT STATE OF MISSOURI, KNOWN AS THE GATEWAY TO THE WEST.

FACT: Thomas Jefferson's vision of the spread of freedom and democracy from "sea to shining sea" inspired Eero Saarinen's masterpiece of modern design. The 630 foot stainless steel Gateway Arch reflects St. Louis' role as the gateway to the West. The Arch stands 630 feet (192 m) tall, and is 630 feet (192 m) wide at its base. It is the tallest habitable structure in St. Louis, and the second tallest in Missouri.

A/ARCH

Tuned City

Tuned City – between sound and space speculation – was an exhibition and conference project in Berlin which proposed a new evaluation of architectural spaces from the perspective of their acoustic qualities.

The poster series was printed on a 5 colour offset machine loaded with 5 pantone special colours. The printer was allowed to use his heidelberg printing press like a musical instrument – switching the single colour units on and off in order to create a broad variety of overprint effects and many different posters in one go.

Design: Andreas Tšpfer, Michael Rudolph, Carsten Stabenow

Client: Tuned City Plattform for Sound and Architecture

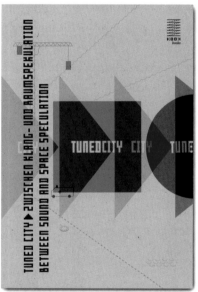

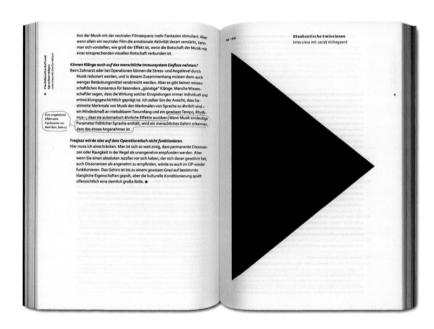

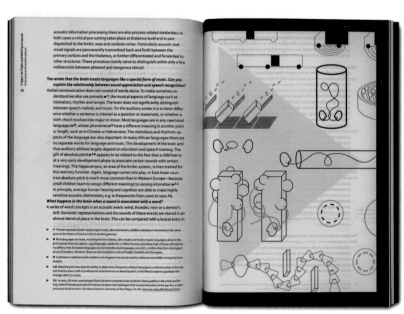

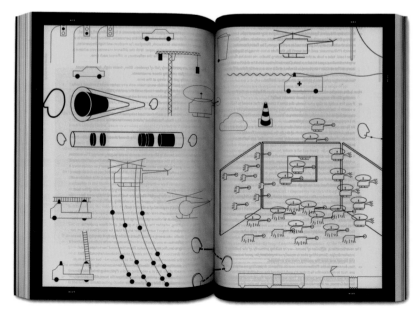

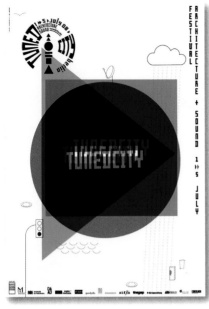
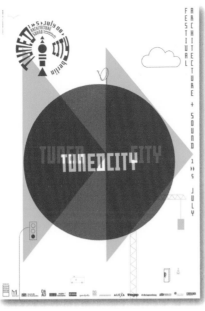

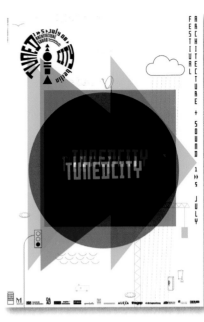
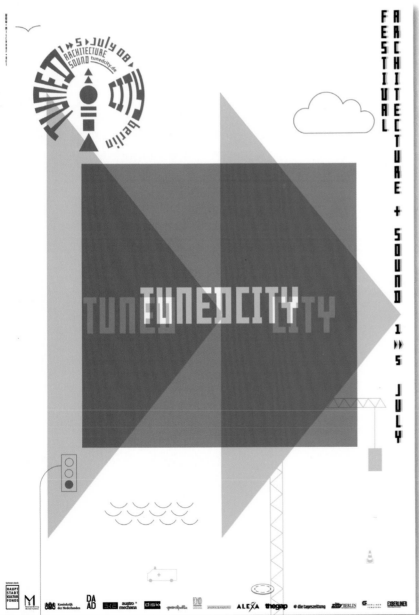
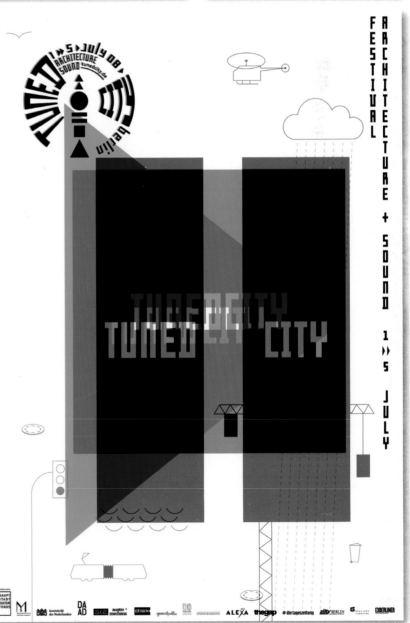

Playlab

Identity and stationery for Playlab, a workshop space aimed to be a creative playground for stressed adults. The Illustrations used are a mixture of scientific elements and random fun images. The stationery is printed in fluorescent Pantone colours while the actual logo is simply blind embossed. The address details are filled in using a rubber stamp.

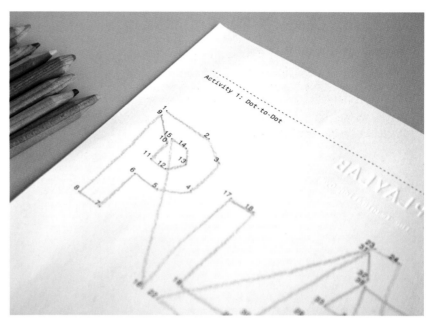

Activity 1: Dot-to-Dot

Pål Laukli

"The last thing I want is some minimal, so-phisticated bullshit," was Pål's insightful brief to Mission. Pål is known for his fast & loose approach to shoots, so the designers tried to capture that personal energy in his identity. They combined retro camera manuals, comic books and various stuff from Pål's world, which was then printed in "minimal" fluorescent pink on "unsophisticated" card board.

PÅL LAUKLI >> PORTFOLIO

Mission

Wildlife

When working on client projects the designers at Mission occasionaly come up with concepts and ideas that do not necessarily fit the client's brief, but still have great potential. "Wildlife" is one such idea.

Mission chose to invest quite some time on this project, which they worked on in collaboration with the photographer Pål Laukli. It turned out to be a project they are very proud of.

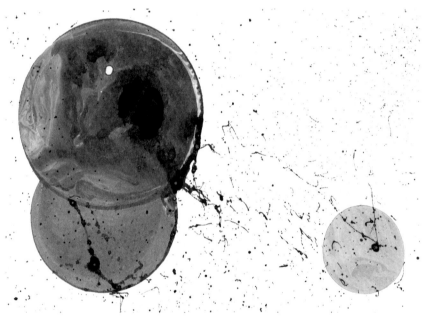

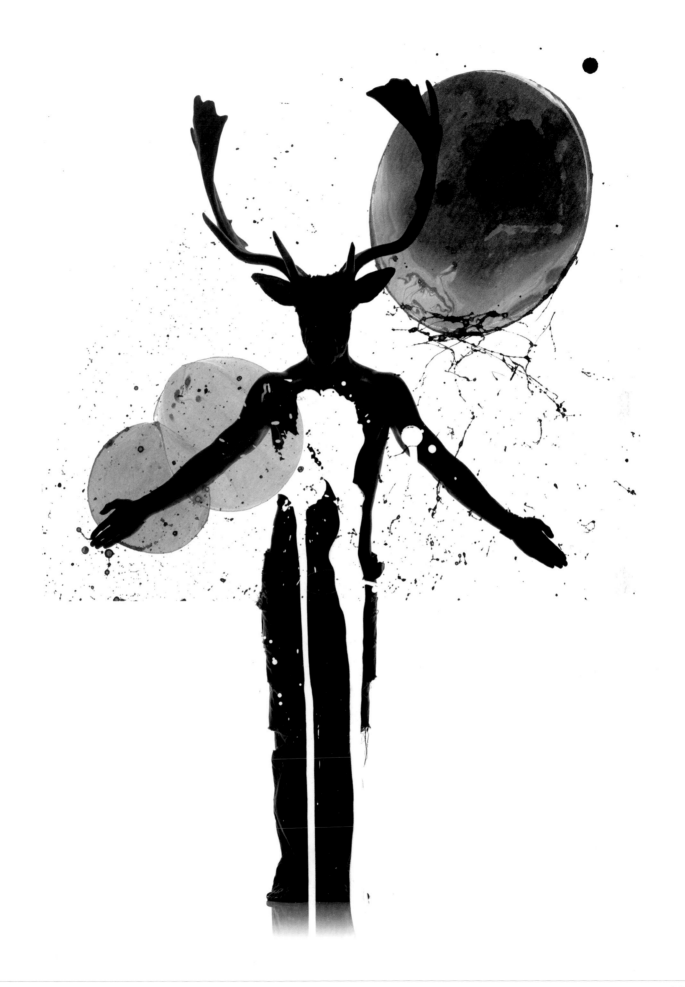

The Norwegian National Museum

Many museums have traditionally focused more on the collection than the audience, resulting in low visitor numbers. But museums nowadays can´t only be the guardians of national treasures. They need to become attractions.

The new slogan "More than Munch" makes it clear that the museum is moving away from the old "one-collection approach". The identity has a simple typographical style, with just one font and two colours. The wordplay used conveys the great wealth of cultural education that the museum has to offer visitors, as well as giving the museum a more playful image.

Living Identity

'Living Identity' is Moving Brands' first self-initiated paper and expresses their philosophy that brands must be alive to change if they are to thrive in a moving world. The book is divided in two sections. Moving Brands wanted their views to be conveyed with great immediacy, so the first section was printed on Cyclus uncoated stock to give it the feel of notepaper. The second section looks at 'living identities'

that they, as a studio, have created and is printed on gloss stock to give full effect to the images. The cover is a 12-page gate fold and acts as a 'reveal' for the project timeline, that spans eleven years of their history.

To help the book 'live' beyond its printed form, the designers made their logo – featured on the book's cover – into a marker for Augmented Reality (AR) technology. The marker is read

by a webcam and, in conjunction with a web browser application, launches the AR. They assigned four different web feeds to the four orientations of the cover. 90 and 270 degrees (portrait) are feeds from their blog and Twitter respectively, 0 and 180 degrees (landscape) draw Flickr and Vimeo feeds of their work. As each of these feeds are constantly updated, the user will see the studio's latest views and work.

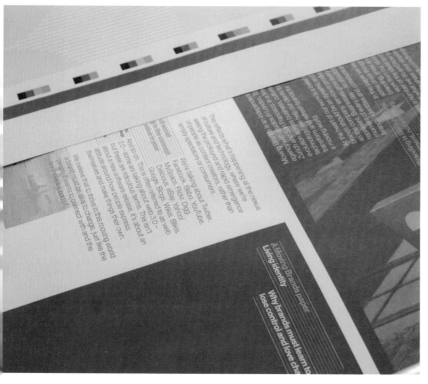

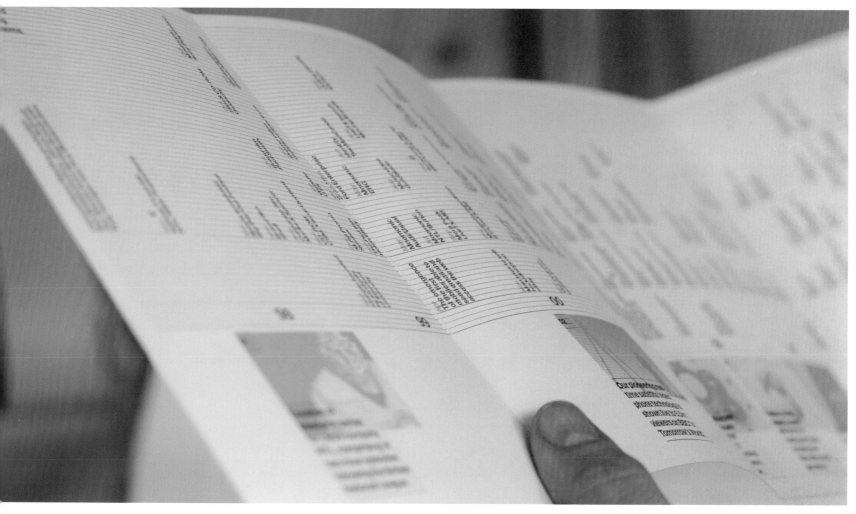

MyORB stationery

New branding and identity for MyORB, an arts
and design practice in New York City.

*Pencils/
Product*

Hail to the Pencil

In 1950 Astronauts realized that their pens were not working in space.
The Americans spent billions of dollars to develop a pen that would
work in zero gravity. The Russians used a pencil. Hail to the pencil!
The great thing about them is that they change through use and
sharpening. Sold in Sets of 3. $5.

4 Options:

*Mix, Red,
Orange, Green*

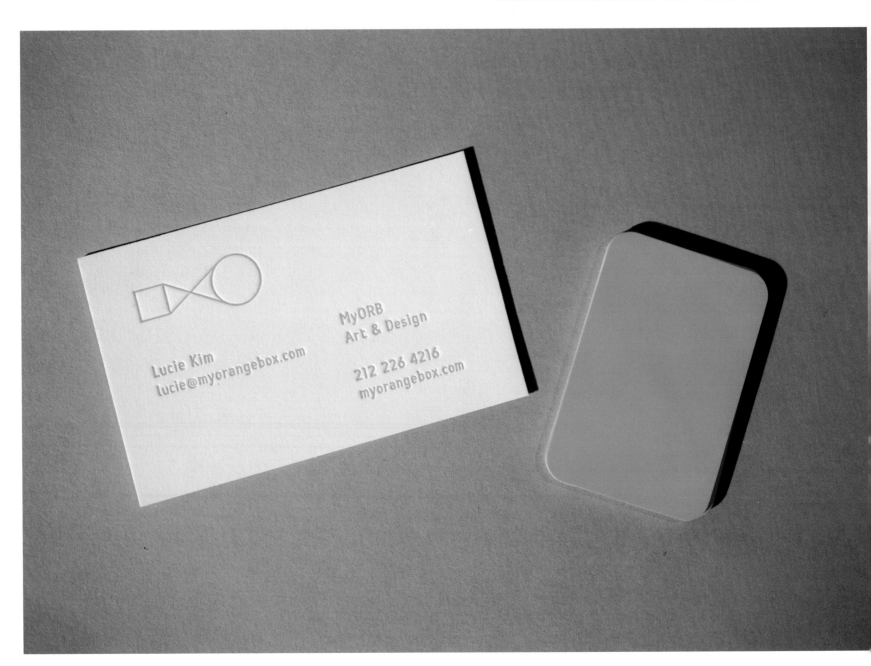

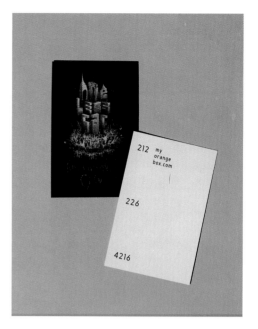

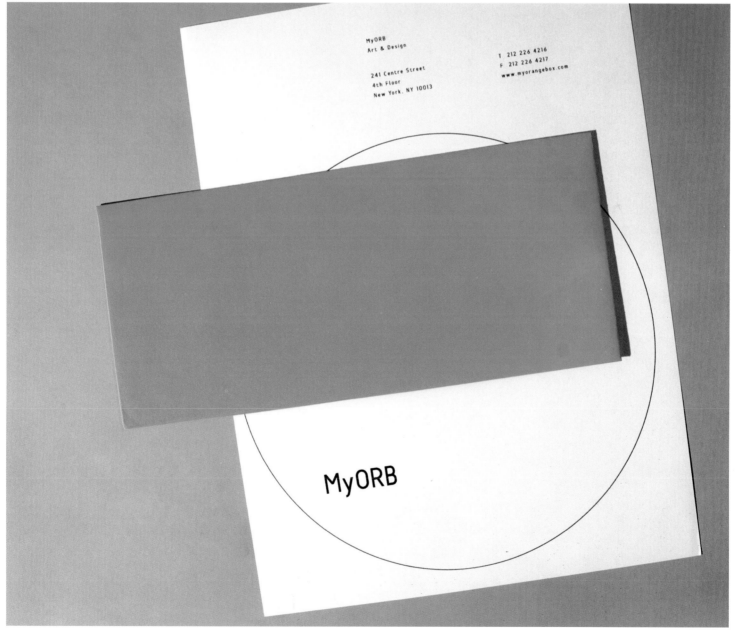

MyORB Issue 2

While lecturing at Parsons Kidi in Japan, Lucie ventured out to document Japanese life and its curiosities. This zine can be directly purchased from the studio.

341 is a gallery and art advisory which is inspired by Alfred Stieglitz's 291. MyORB wanted to make sure that the identity had a contemporary feel and based the system on mathematics.

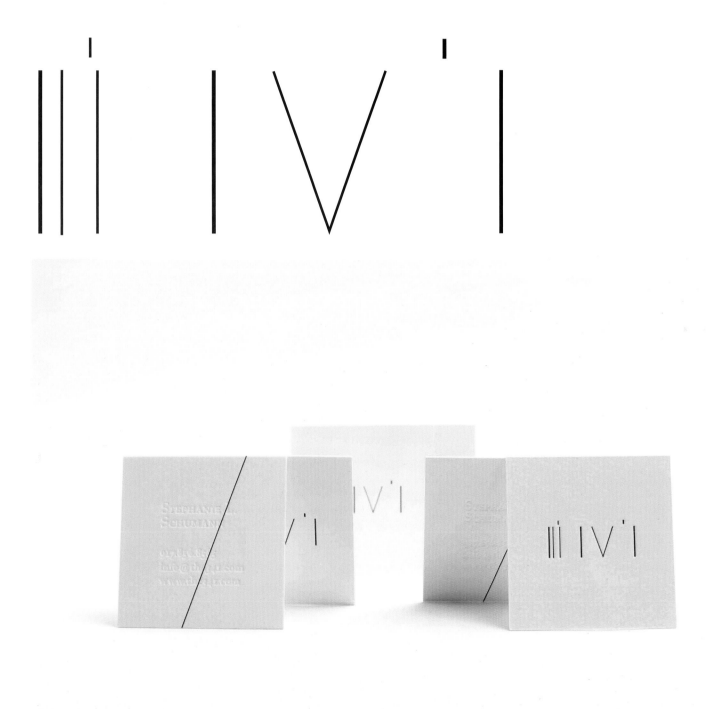

Cause & Effect

For this project, the clients – a video post-production house – were looking for an identity system that demonstrated the cause-and-effect principle in order to make a visual pun on the company's name. They also wanted the identity system to reflect the playful qualities of their collective personalities, a key component to the company's identity that helps distinguish it from its competitors. The designers began by approaching the challenge conceptually. They envisioned the dynamic "cause" as representing the company itself and the "effect" to stand for the work they produced. MyORB wanted to depict the "cause" as a constant entity awaiting the catalyst a client provides. The "effect" is the ensuing alchemy of that relationship; the work being indeterminate and contingent on the specific needs of each client and project.

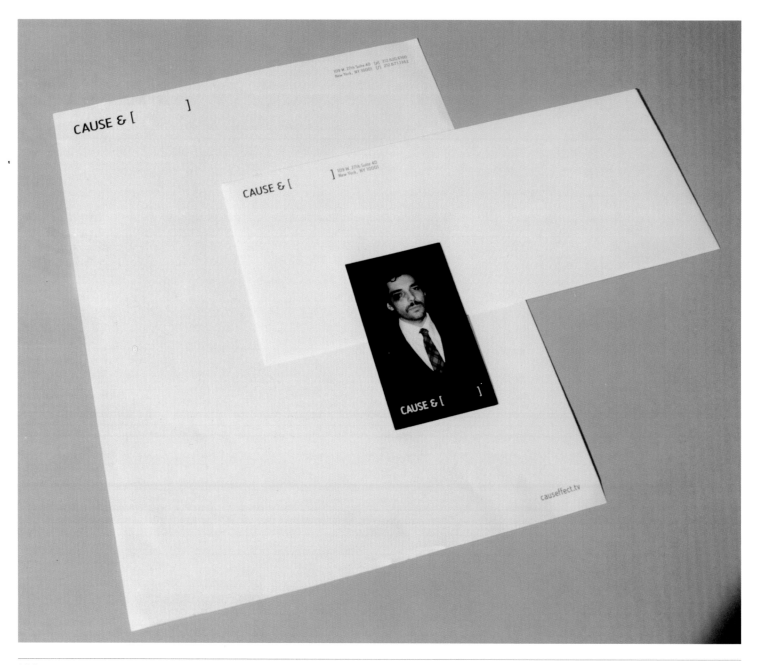

Cherner

New branding and identity for an arts and design practice in New York City.

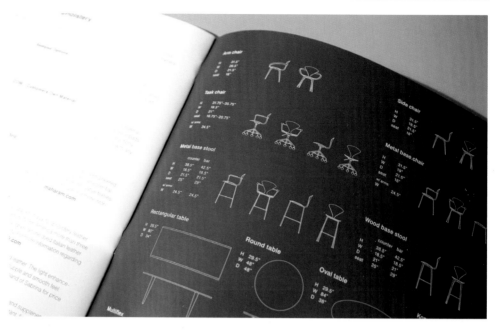

Konwiser table

Norman Cherner, 1958

The Konwiser rectangular table was designed by Norman Cherner in 1958 and exhibited at The Museum of Modern Art's *Good Design* Exhibition. The sheet-and-chrome-base-table 24" solid stainless steel arms which are matched into the table top. The moulded top has a 1" solid edge band and a core 4"-1/8" thick plywood/plywood. Konwiser tables are available in 72" and 60" lengths. Made in the U.S.A.

"Form follows function has been misunderstood. Form and function should be one."
— Frank Lloyd Wright

Metal base stool

Norman Cherner, 1958

Metal base stools are ideal for the home or for bar/cafe/restaurant settings. Available in counter height, with or without upholstered seats. Stools have moulded plywood and chromed steel. Matches with a high-chrome base solid armrest on a single chrome arc. Reduced from the original drawings and prints. Cherner metal base stool. An easy, lightweight and fits the highest. Made in the U.S.A.

"Organic design seeks superior sense of use and a free sense of comfort, expressed in organic simplicity."
— Frank Lloyd Wright

Cherner
The Cherner Chair Company

ChernerChair.com
toll free 866. 243.7637

Children's Classroom Furniture by Benjamin Cherner

50 YEARS Cherner

ChernerChair.com
toll free 866. 243.7637

Cherner
The Cherner Chair Company

ChernerChair.com
toll free 866. 243.7637

Tube Table and Tube Floor Lamps by Norman Cherner (1958)

Daimler Contemporary

The brief was to create an exhibition leaflet for two simultaneous exhibitions with overlapping themes in the Daimler Contemporary in Berlin. The circles and type are hand drawn and the two colours used in the design help to differentiate the details of each exhibition and identify the that works are included in both. As both exhibitions were held over the same period of time and were based around similar subjects, the idea of intersecting and overlapping circles seemed appropriate to represent the overlap of the exhibitions. To accommodate the tight funding and the two exhibitions coinciding with one another, it was natural for the leaflets and posters fro the two exhibitions to be combined in one printwork.

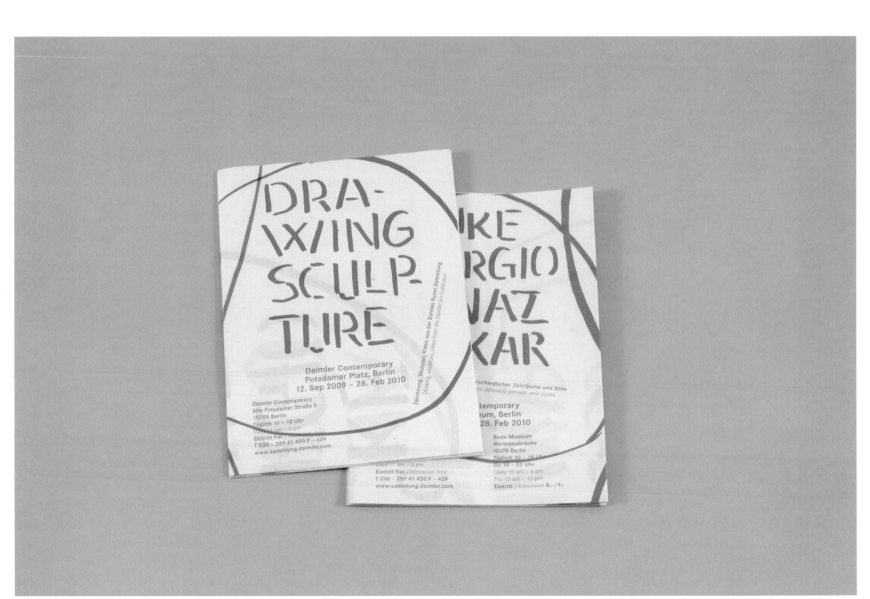

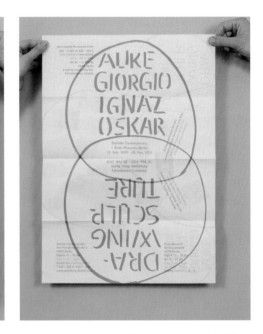

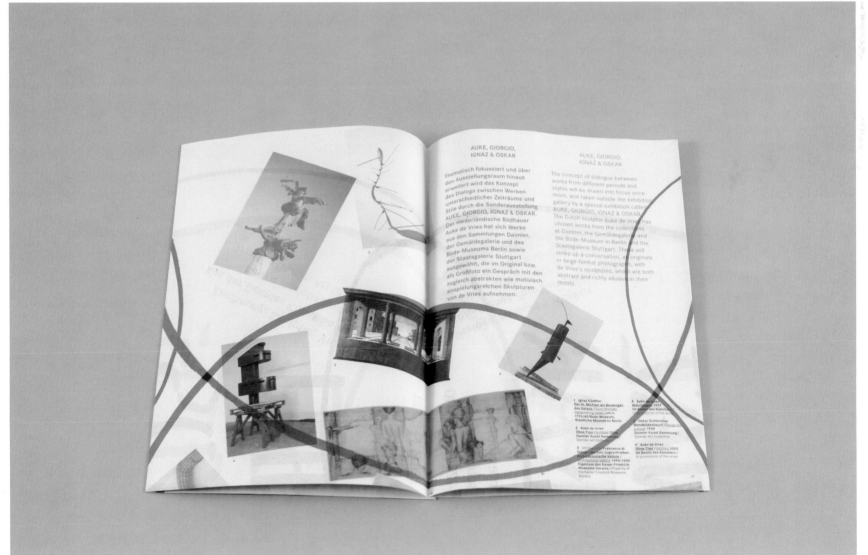

Droomintendant

Looking for someone able to make a contribution to the cultural diversity within the arts, the Fonds BKVB organised a presentation and a debate under the title 'De Droomintendant'. The theme of 'cultural diversity' was represented in the brochure by patterns based on a mix of flags. These patterns were combined with the letters of the titles.

The brochure consists of four parts, each in its own size (invitation, general project information, an artistic intervention and an overview of 47 plans), but which are united through the titles and colours. Each letter and digit got its own pattern, thus creating an alphabet of patterns, based on flags.

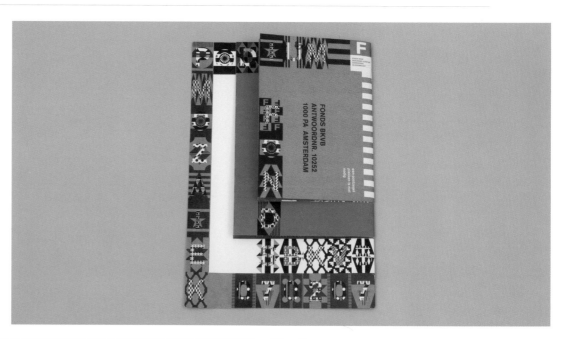

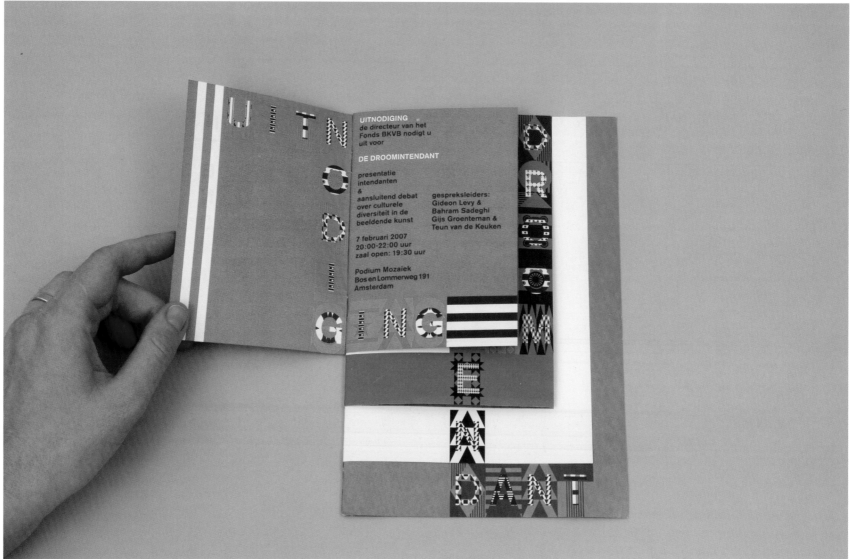

Substitut is a non-profit exhibition space with the mission of presenting Swiss artists in Berlin. The name is composed of 'subculture' and 'institute' and indicates the mixed nature of the venue. onlab's main principle for the corporate identity was to play with typography in a non-Swiss way, i.e. free as opposed to strict and playful as opposed to formal.

Inspired by the unfinished wall surfaces in the gallery's interior that reveal the space's past, the typography is built on two layers: only when the two layers come together do they reveal the content of the exhibition. The element of decoding and unveiling is suggestive of Substitute's unfinished and evolving nature.

Art Direction, Design: onlab, Nicolas Bourquin and Thibaud Tissot
Type Design: Thibaud Tissot

ABCDEFGHIJKLM
NOPQRSTUVWXYZ

TM-City

The exhibition TM-City, held in La Chapelle, Chaumont, France, mapped the work of Richard Niessen in a city landscape where over 150 of his works were presented as architecture. TM-City consisted of eight city-quarters, each with their own type of works; in 'Calligraphic Quarter' for instance, the typography echoed the seamless integration of calligraphy, imagery and text found in Byzantine and Medieval illuminated manuscripts. The other quarters were: Structures Citadel; Alphabet Block; Flows and Ruptures; Patternville; Sugarcraft Hill; The Collaboration; and Toolkits Treasure. The exhibition was designed as a travelling exhibition; after Chaumont it went to Stedelijk Museum Amsterdam and KOP in Breda, and in 2009 travelled to Vilnius and Sofia. TM-City could be taken apart and fitted into eight crates. In the printed material surrounding the different exhibitions, the structure of the streets was overlaid at different scales, thus creating a dynamic graphic pattern.

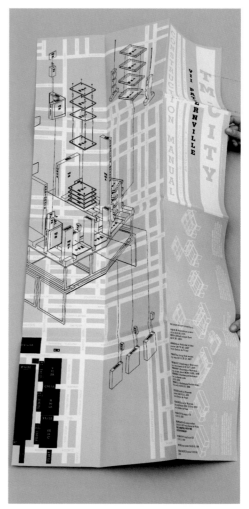

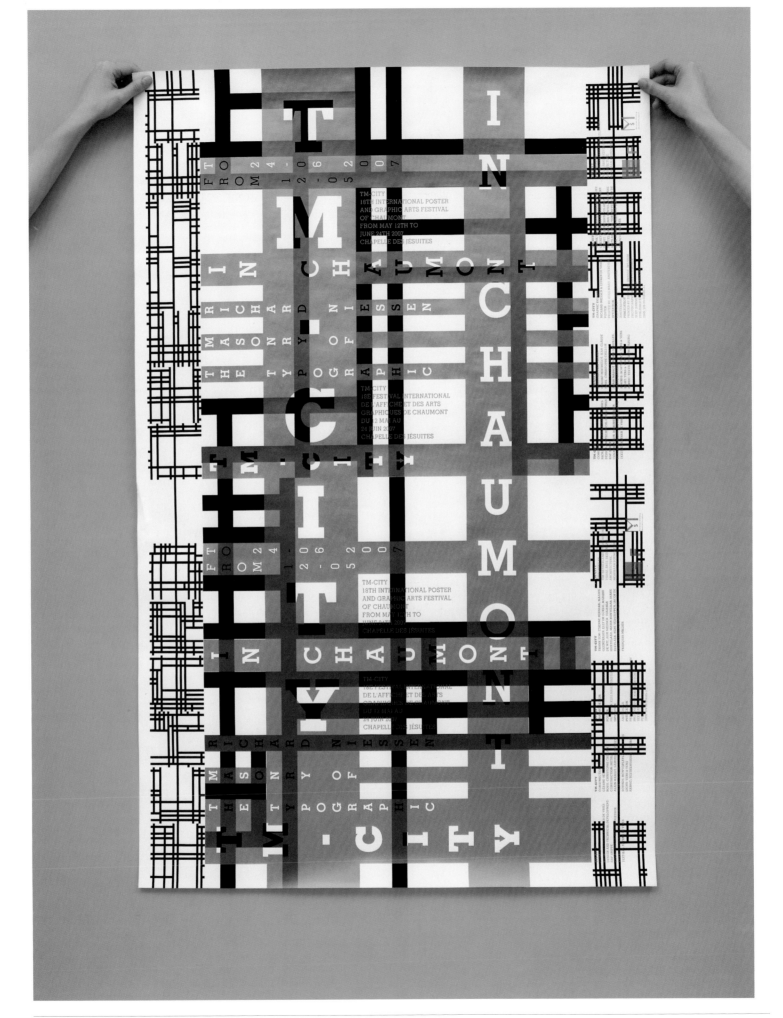

GYÁR

GYÁR is a Budapest-based post production studio founded in 2005. They decided to celebrate their 5th anniversary with a fresh new company look. Official Classic had the pleasure of working for them on the project.

The designers' task was to create a brand new company logo and identity and redesign GYÁR's website, blog and newsletter.

They also had to do some illustrations for the big empty studio walls. The result was six A0-sized posters and 4 wall paintings.

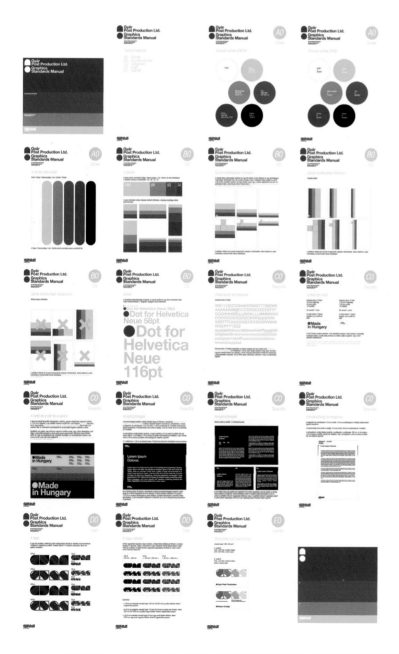

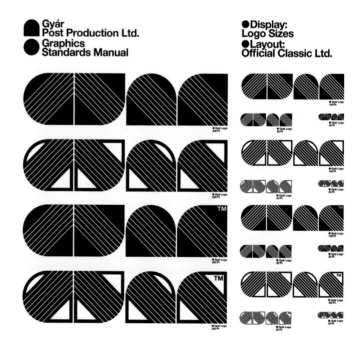

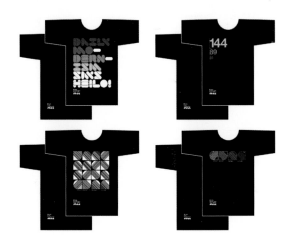

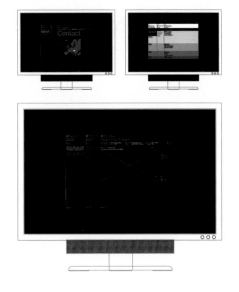

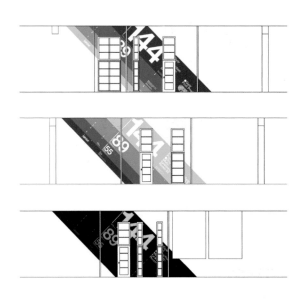

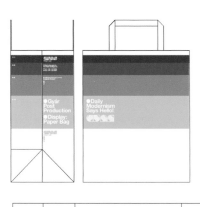

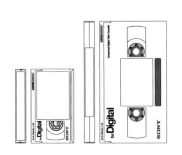

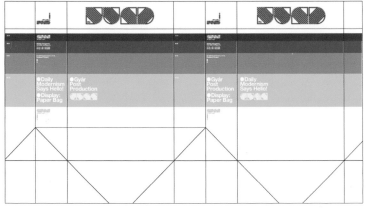

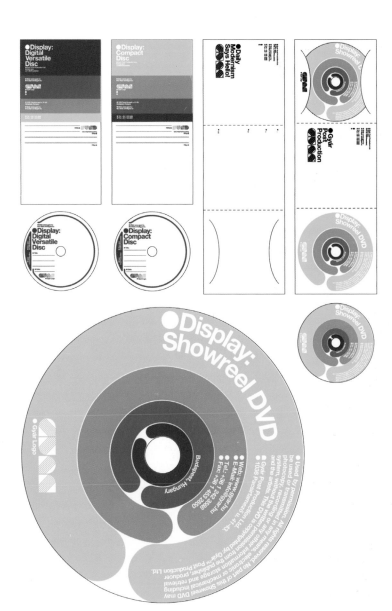

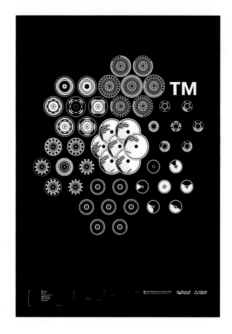

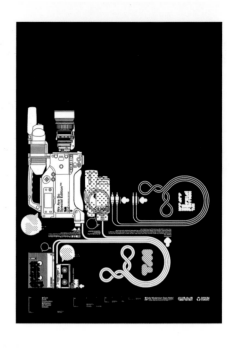

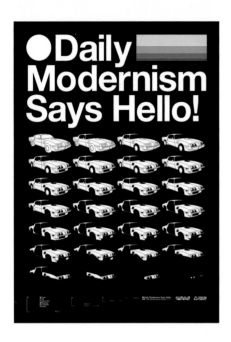

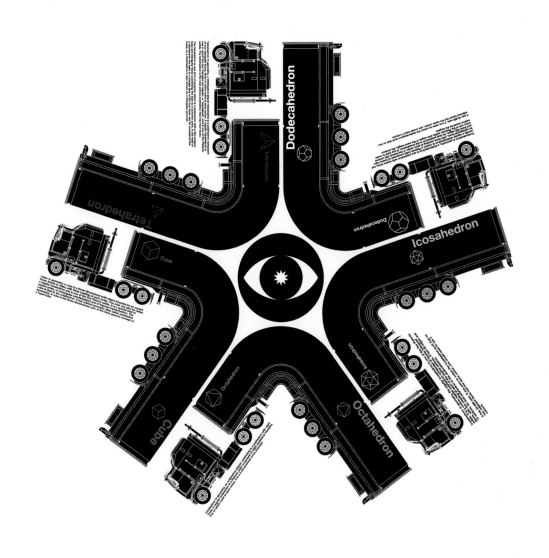

●Daily Modernism Says Hello!

OFFICIN CLASSIC

HypeForType

Official Classic were asked by Alex Haigh – Thinkdust to do a proposal work / case study for his HypeForType project. The brief was to create a new logo for HFT which would work with the existing website. The designers also had to demonstrate various ways in which the logo could be used for different branding purposes such as promoting the typefaces from the HFT library.

The Making of Your Magazines

onlab's concept for the exhibition 'The Making of Your Magazines' offered two approaches to the 40 years' history of discourse in the magazine archplus. The thematic development of the magazine was presented in the form of a long information graphic on the wall which chronologically mapped the evolution of 12 selected topics. The second approach engaged the visitors in compiling their own selection of articles from the past 40 years to create their own issue of archplus.

The entire exhibition design was based on DIN A4 format using 6 different paper colors and a low-tech b/w copy machine.

As for the production of their magazines, visitors would find folders with all selected articles right by the copy machine. While the editors were working on the latest issue, copies were to be stapled between two cardboard sheets, one being the cover with the archplus logo and the other one being the backcover. Visitors could fold the exhibition poster into a cover for their magazine and place the copied articles inside.

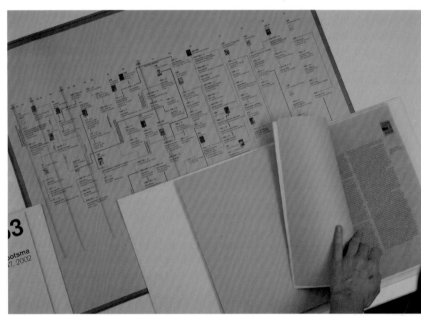

Operation Butterfly

Operation Butterfly compresses the content of a company into an essence. They then release the essence allowing for the largest possible impact to unfold. For this purpose, the brand must be experienced emotionally to allow bonding and the formation of a brand-consumer / consumer-brand relationship. Good branding is about good storytelling. Operation Butterfly emotionalizes brands through visual storytelling in order to effectively anchor them in peoples' minds.

The name Operation Butterfly – Effective Branding derives from the butterfly effect: a common illustration used to explain chaos theory. The idea is that small variations in the initial condition of a dynamic system can produce large variations in the long term behavior of the system. The phenomenon was encapsulated by Edward N. Lorenz in 1972 in the question: Can the flap of a butterfly's wings in Brazil set off a tornado in Texas?

Creative direction & design: Balázs Tarsoly

Cody Paulson

Laramie Carlson

Photographer Laramie Carlson asked Cody Paulson to design him a logo, stationery, and a portfolio website. The logo was inspired by a camera lens and the black and white color scheme is symbolic of the sharp, high-contrast photos that Laramie consistently takes. The last unifying element was a hyphen, which was placed at specific proportionate intervals as a play on the word "grapher".

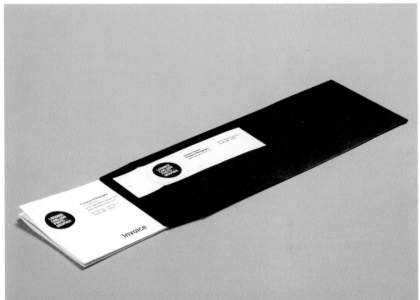

Operation Butterfly

Selected

When Selected Gallery started expanding, Operation Butterfly developed the umbrella brand Selected Concepts with the sub-brands Gallery and Interiors. It is a clear branding that simplifies communication for all upcoming Selected concepts and that holds everything together. At the same time it allows clear differentiation through the use of a colour code and the application of diverse photography styles.

Creative direction & design: Balázs Tarsoly

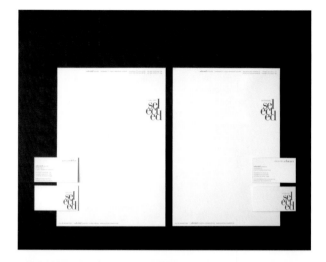

See The Light / Se Lyset

The Danish Design Center's main exhibition of 2009, 'See the Light' was an informative and fascinating exhibition about future lighting design. With an emphasis on sustainability and quality, the exhibition presented the light sources that are available today and explored what light sources the future might bring.

Mads Jakob Poulsen made the identity, invitations, signage and screen animations for the exhibition.

The logo is a play on the title Se lyset, in English See the light. Both title words are contained in one. Furthermore, the logo itself is unreadable without light, as part of the logo in all printed media is printed on the back of the paper. With light the logo is visible in black and grey. The outcome is a unique and simple identity which fits well with the exhibition and leaves room for the exciting visual impressions of the exhibits.

Goodmorning Technology Aps
Att Mads Jakob Poulsen
Vestergade 12 A 1
1456 København K

PP DANMARK

 INVITATION

SE   T∃ƨY⅃

Dansk Design Center inviterer Dem med ledsager til åbning
af udstillingen

SE LYSET
Fredag den 30. januar 2009 kl 16.00 - 18.00

Belysning gennemgår i disse år en omfattende forandring - og
det mest markante eksempel er den velkendte glødepære, der
i flere lande er blevet forbudt. Det betyder, at det lys vi er vant
til at se vores arbejde, mad og hinanden i, vil ændre sig.

Udviklingen rummer store udfordringer for belysningsbranchen,
og den kan skabe inspiration til spændende nytænkning - en
nødvendighed i alle brancher.

SE LYSET viser de lyskilder vi har til rådighed i dag, og med
afsæt i de nyeste teknologier, designs og produkter fortæller
12 eksperter om nye innovative og energibesparende mulig-
heder indenfor belysning.

Udstillingen omfatter tre udstillingsområder:
"Se Lyset" i stueetagen, "Styr Lyset" på 1. sal og i underetagen
vises lysinstallationen "Interference".

Talere:
Introduktion ved direktør Kenneth Munck, Dansk Center for Lys
Hovedtaler og åbning ved videnskabsminister Helge Sander

Med venlig hilsen,
Dansk Design Center

Christian Scherfig
Adm direktør

DDC°

Dansk Design Center
Danish Design Centre

DDC°

Dansk Design Center
Danish Design Centre

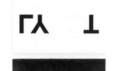

Central Saint Martins

Central Saint Martins College of Art and Design provides unrivalled opportunities which enable students to realise their potential and make a significant contribution to the 21st century. The college produces a large amount of marketing materials, from the main college prospectus to short course campaigns, and exhibitions showcasing the best of students' work.

Three years ago, the college chose Praline to look after their internal and external communication, student recruitment material and exhibition graphics. Creativity was to be at the heart of the college communication, reflecting Central Saint Martins' excellency in design and communication. Since being appointed, Praline has worked very closely with both the College Marketing and the Short Courses departments to consistently produce inspiring material.

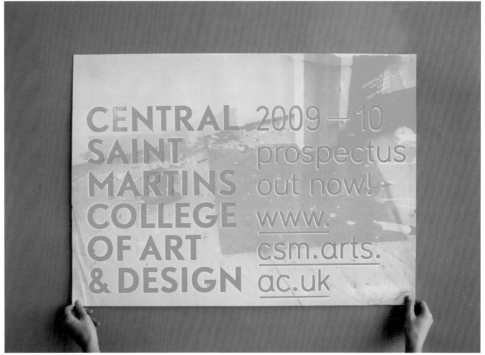

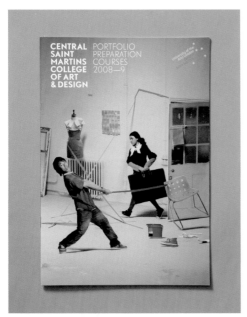

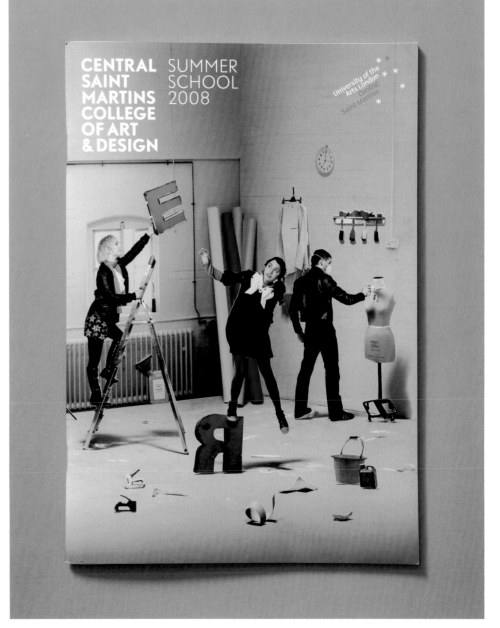

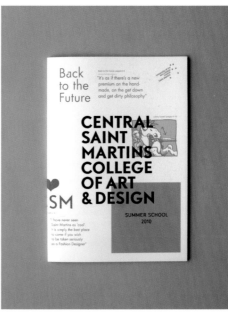

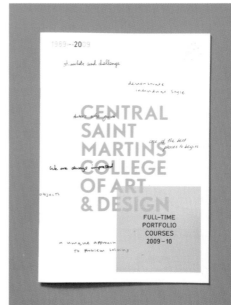

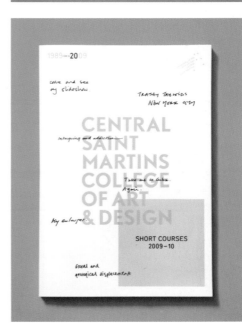

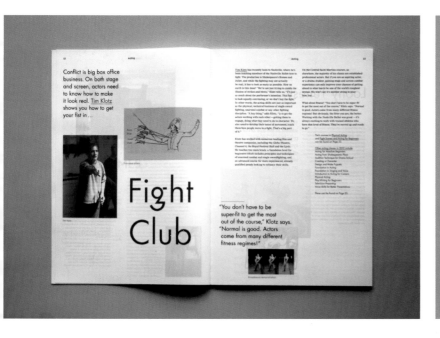

I ♥ CSM

What excites you about the fashion scene in London?
London is the perfect place to develop a creative style without commercial constraint. The difference between London, Paris and New York is that New York is very industrialized and commercial: study there and you will be pushed in that direction. Paris has a high-end boutique/couture emphasis. London is not high-end; it's High Street. It's a very broad place to come and study.

When you want to be inspired where do you go?
It all depends on the project, but I virtually live in the Victoria & Albert Museum, British Museum and the Tate! They are all fantastic.

Which London shop do you find most difficult to walk past without popping in?
I am a sucker for Liberty and Dover Street Market. They are both very beautiful and very 'London'.

Which young British designer should we all be looking out for?
Holly Foulton. I love her embellishments and silhouettes. I am a big fan.

What's your favourite outfit?
I am a total slob I'm afraid, so it's a pair of Dexter Wong Jeans and a Rick Owens T-shirt.

If you could wipe out one current fashion trend, what would it be?
Diversity is the backbone of design. As soon as you start dictating you create conformity.

What inspired you to become a fashion designer?
I was lucky enough to be at John Galliano's debut show, way back when.

Why is Central Saint Martins so cool?
I have never seen Central Saint Martins as 'cool'. It is simply the best place to come if you wish to be taken seriously as a Fashion Designer.

Why do so many students come to the Summer School each year?
Summer School's great. You can take a class with some of the best in the business.

What's your biggest fashion disaster?
One man's fashion disaster is another man's dream …

Is fashion important?
Not at all, and absolutely (take your pick!)

Ian's courses for Summer 2010:
Building a Fashion Collection
Designing a Commercial Fashion Collection
Introduction to Fashion Design.

Our fashion and textile courses also cover computing, accessories, illustration, marketing and making, both in the studios and workshops of our Charing Cross Road, Soho and Southampton Row, Holborn sites.

All fashion and textile classes appear on Pages 19 to 22 of the Course Listings.

"I have never seen Saint Martins as 'cool'. It is simply the best place to come if you wish to be taken seriously as a Fashion Designer"

All images from the School of Fashion and Textiles at Central Saint Martins

Join the list of students and staff alumni that includes:
Jeff Banks, Antonio Berardi, Robert Cary-Williams, Hussein Chalayan, Joyce Clissold, Terence Conran, Giles Deacon, John Galliano, Katharine Hamnett, Stephen Jones, Stella McCartney, Alexander McQueen, Bruce Oldfield, Rifat Ozbek, Edvardo Paolozzi, Phoebe Philo, Clements Ribeiro, Tristan Webber and Matthew Williamson.

What's the best thing about studying fashion in London?
We asked fashion designer Ian Scott Kettle, who graduated from Central Saint Martins and completed an MA at the Royal College of Art. He launched his own womenswear label in 2008 and is a regular, busy tutor at Central Saint Martins Summer School.

POBEDA

For the identity of POBEDA gallery, a photography gallery in Moscow, Praline designed a cyrillic alphabet based on Glaser Stencil.

They chose Glaser for its directness and simplicity as a stencil font. The stencil font echoed the character of the refurbished industrial building where the gallery was located. It also offered possibilities for stencilling on walls and die cutting text into invitations and other printed materials.

The cyrillic characters follow the drawings of the original font and adapt the cut lines to the russian characters. It was important to keep the same feel and to make sure the new letters would feel like part of the Glaser family. It was especially interesting for the designers to develop a cyrillic font as none of them speak russian. The client was extremely pleased and apparently Russian speakers find it somehow amusing and odd!

POBEDA FONT

ABCDEFGHJKLMNOPQRSTUVWXYZ
0123456789
АБВГДЕЖЗИЙКЛМНОПРСТУФХЦЧ
ШЩЪЫЬЭЮЯ

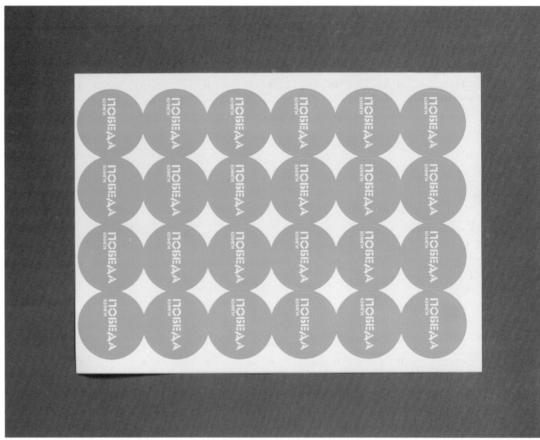

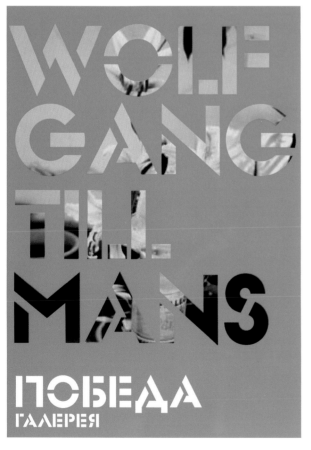

Research Center for Fashion, the Body and Material Cultures

Such a long name! The designers at Praline used it as a rock on which to found the whole identity. The shape of the name became the logo: the cut-out window through which images are shown, and the individual mark of a 'cutting-edge' (!) department of the University of the Arts London.

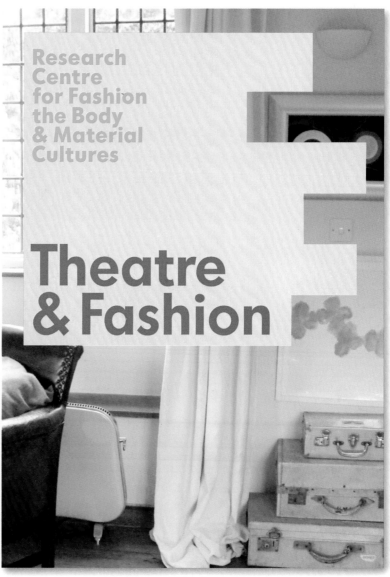

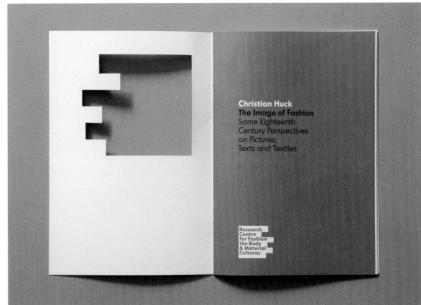

Raffinerie

Daros

Daros is dedicated to the collection and exhibition of contemporary European and pan-American art. Raffinerie have been handling the broad range of print productions for a number of years now, delivering everything from corporate design to exhibition catalogues. Each individual exhibition is supported by a tailor-made design solution.

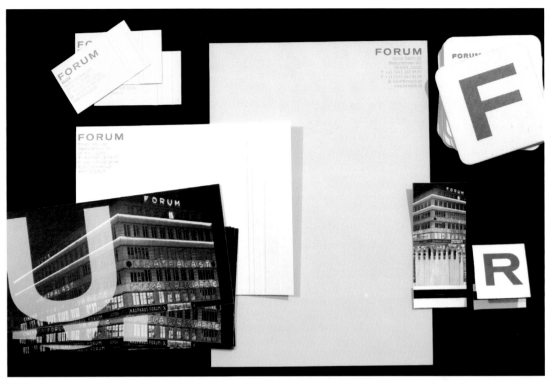

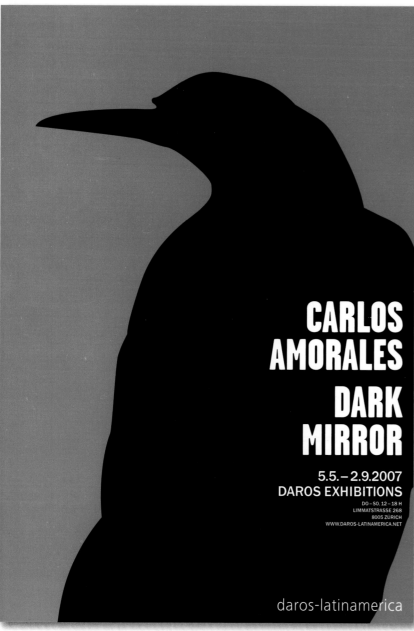

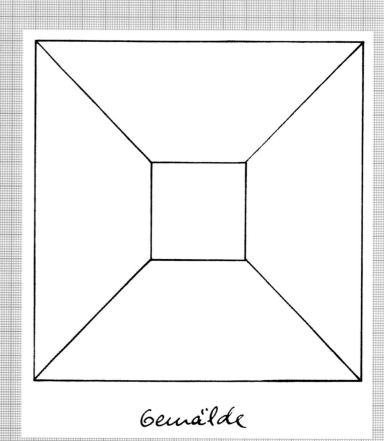

DSVC Rough

When Range volunteered to create a monthly issue of Rough for the Dallas Society of Visual Communications, they wanted to do something that had never been done before. This required the team at Range to investigate numerous possibilities and criteria for the publication. They decided to create a piece that redefined what it actually means to be sustainable. The result was a unique book that was efficient in size, used soy based inks, incorporated recycled papers, and utilized FSC certified printing techniques. The innovative use of perforated French fold binding techniques on the outside edge of the book allowed the user to open up the hidden pages and discover the 14 month calendar inside which featured handy tips on how to live a sustainable life. The calendar and daily tools sprinkled throughout this issue added entertainment value and infinite shelf life.

Designer: Garrett Owen, Josh Ege, Maya Kwan
Illustrator: Garrett Owen, Josh Ege
Creative Director: John Swieter
Photographer: Jeremy Sharp
Writer: Shannon Catlett, Mark Fake, Derek Rundgren, Jeremy Sharp, Garrett Owen, Josh Ege

Hybrid

Hybrid, a Dallas-based design and interactive agency founded by Range creator John Swieter, was an industry-leading example of the modern professional work environment. Hybrid's offices were a collaboration between GFF Architects, Herman Miller and Hybrid Design Director and CEO John Swieter. The goal was to create a brand-centric work environment that incorporated all aspects of technology, workflow and human interaction. The result was an award-winning environment that captured the culture and distinctive design sense of Hybrid.

Designer: John Swieter
Architects: Brian Kuper, GFF, Craig Beneke,
AF Architecture and Fabrication
Creative Director: John Swieter
Writer: Wayne Geyer

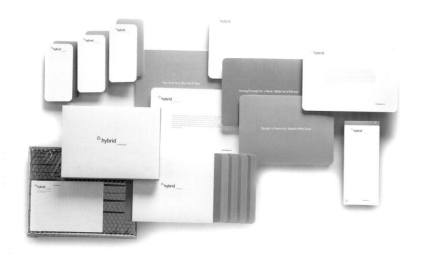

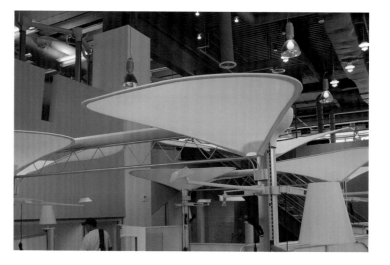

The Gina Zeidler brand was created for the Minnesota, USA, photographer with a balance of shabby chic, vintage and clean-contemporary. The sophisticated brand was developed keeping in mind each step a client would go through, from the letterpressed business cards and pocket folder brochure, to the final delivery of digital images on disk, and the prints in the screenprinted fabric bag that is personalized with a multi-layer tag and a polaroid from the event. Using a calligrapher, Red Organic were able to create a unique type treatment for the logo mark. The plume icon and pattern on the fabric bag tie the brand together with layered texture. The designers utilized several different techniques including letterpress, digital printing and screenprinting to achieve the full brand package.

Design and layout for the anniversary issue of
a Finnish poetry magazine.

Roycroft Design

Bette Troy Stationary

Elegance, personality, and attention to detail describe the work of photo stylist Bette Troy. Roycroft Design kept these elements in mind when crafting her logo, business card and stationery.

Poster for a new film production to promote a screening at The Alamo Drafthouse Austin, Texas USA.
Inspired by three key characters whose lives become irreparably tangled.

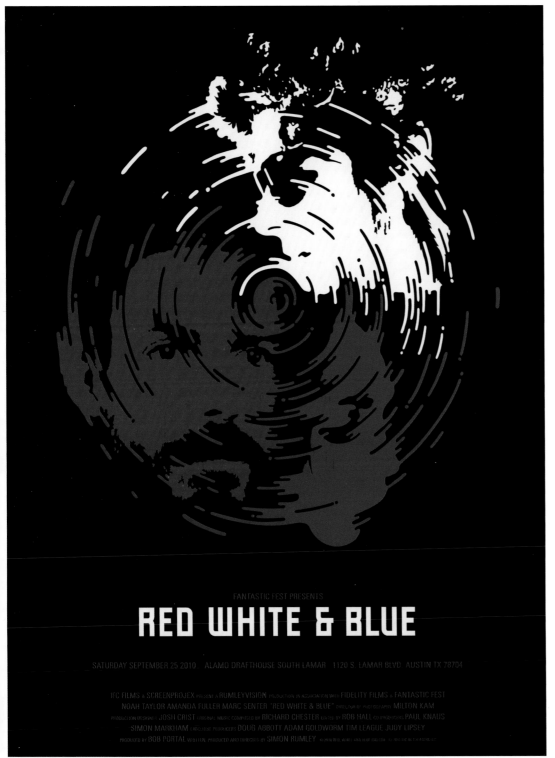

mediaPro

mediaPro have quite a complex message that they wanted to communicate through an innovative piece of print. They wanted to publicise an up-coming event that they were organising, and to introduce their new visual identity. Their message is about the strength of integrated marketing communications — ultimately, integration of communications in a digital age.

Printed material needs to work harder now than ever before because it needs to prove its worth in an ever evolving digital world. With that in mind, the designers at Sawdust wanted to produce something that would be an experience when held and used. This led to the idea of pages that, when overlaid, integrated to reveal a message encouraging the user to engage and interact with what they're holding.

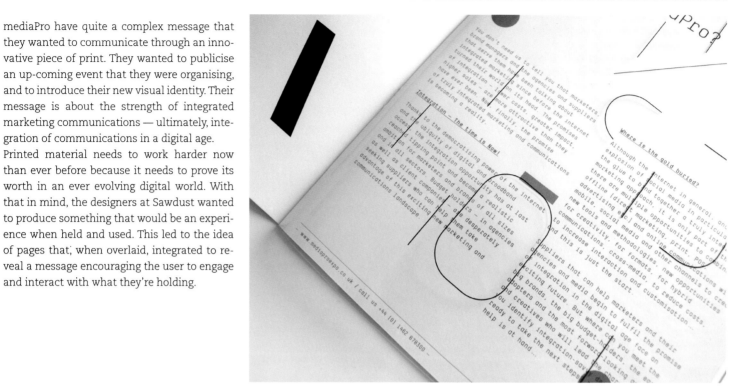

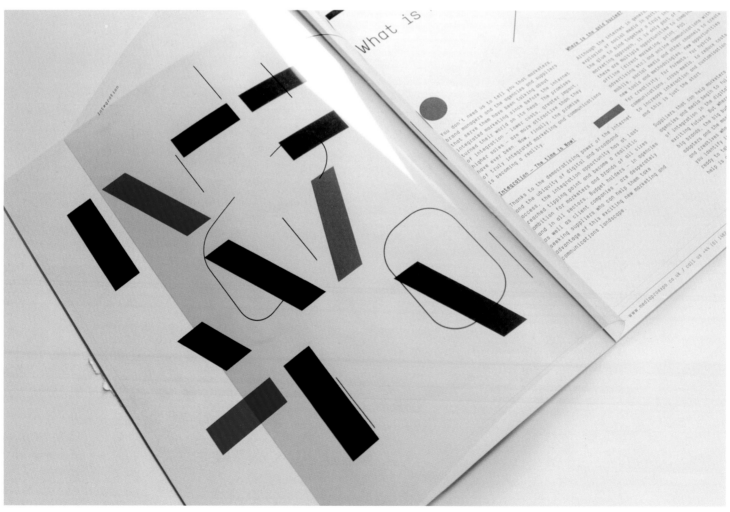

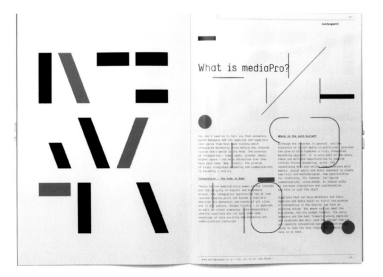

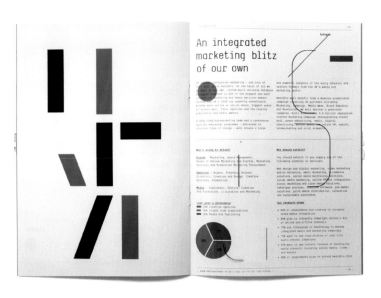

SIGN* greetings tape

Awarded at Type Director Club of NYC 2009 - Typographic Excellence.

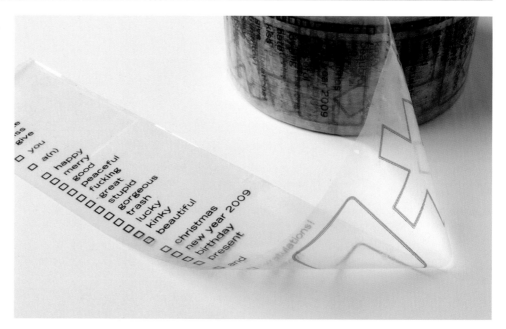

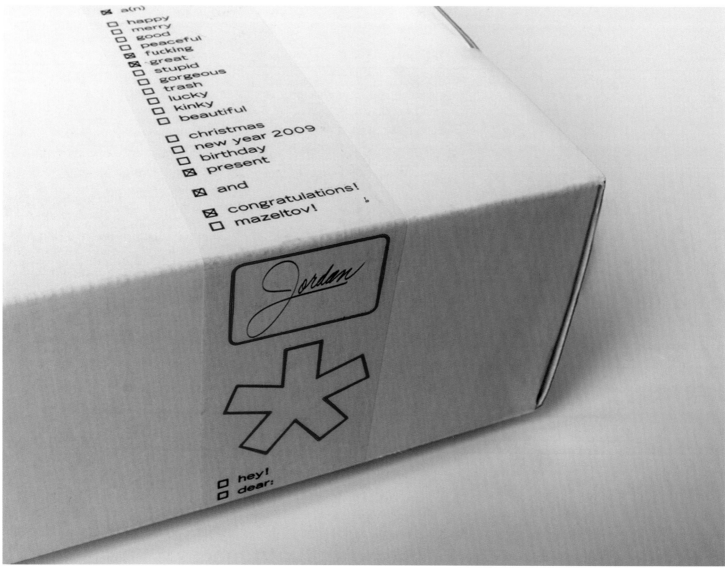

Identity design and buisness cards for Sabatini Architects.

Ginny

Ginny is a contemporary, residential architecture firm that creates custom living spaces. Their personal approach brings years of experience and a breadth of knowledge to bear on every single detail involved in creating spaces that are both functional and beautiful. Spunk was honored to collaborate with the owner and founder, Ginny Anderson, to create this new brand identity.

Creative Director: Jeff Johnson
Senior Designer: Andrew Voss

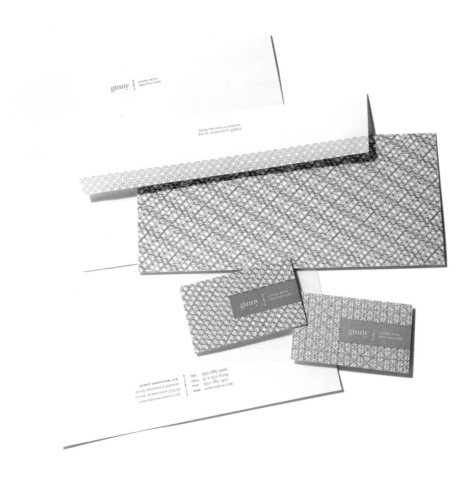

IFP

IFP, the nation's oldest and largest non-profit organization of independent filmmakers, supports the production of 7,000 films, provides resources to more than 20,000 filmmakers, and serves as an advocacy group for the industry. Having grown exponentially in only a few decades, the organization needed a new identity to reflect its relevance and potency in the filmmaking world. Anke Stohlmann Design began by modernizing the original logo and creating consistency of typefaces and color palette across the sub-brands. The look is bold but innately human with fun, poignant details. The system as a whole is intended to be clearly recognizable but also flexible so that as the organization grows and changes, new identity components can be added with ease and consistency. The designers were also conscious of the client's budget, creating a 2-color system that would be inexpensive to print without sacrificing legibility and clarity of message.

Leesa O'Reilly, a stylist, recently expanded her business beyond photographic styling to include product sourcing and location scouting. Additionally, she has also launched a prop hire arm to her business of which all her unique products acquired over the years can be sourced.

Her brandmark is based on the idea that she is constantly sourcing objects from different places. We chose to produce four different business cards to show the diversity of her work and business.

Creative Director: Tim Sutherland
Designer: Elise Lampe
Printer: Bambra Press

LEESA O'REILLY

STYLING
SOURCING
PROPS HIRE

0407 696 372
leesa@leesaoreilly.com.au
leesaoreilly.com.au

Studio Brave

Mike Long Photography

Studio Brave's approach when creating Mike Long's image was to avoid all photographic clichés and most importantly use no photography. This was achieved through raw, uncluttered typography.

Marc Buckner Photography

Each time Marc briefs Studio Brave on a new project a buzz of energy fills the studio. From designing his identity to a series of publications showcasing his work, the designers always find it exciting to see how far they can push things to create an outstanding result. While working collaboratively with Marc on his latest book, the project was open to the designers' interpretation. The freedom to explore and re-interpret the imagery allowed them to showcase his photography in a non-commercial context.

Creative Director: Tim Sutherland
Designers: Katrina Tesoriero, Elise Lampe
Photography: Marc Buckner

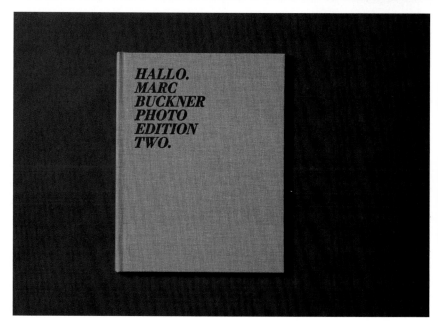

AIGA

Thematically conceptualized and administratively supervised, the AIGA San Diego Y Conference was branded consistently in every way possible. Online promotion, printed collateral and wayfinding was strategized around the conference's sustainable focus. Carbon offsets, recycled printed materials, and mass transit opportunities identified solutions for future events that would yield maximum promotion and minimal natural resource impact.

Art Director: David Conover
Designer: Nate Yates
Copywriter: David Conover
Client: AIGA San Diego

Studio On Fire

2008 Design Camp Materials

Design camp is a well attended weekend event by AIGA Minnesota. These materials reflect the camp theme "Change is coming to the woods". Fictional animals were created and letterpress printed in bright florescent colors.

Designers, Photography: Studio On Fire
Illustrators: Jenna Brouse, Erik Hamline
Writer: Riley Kane
Client: AIGA Minnesota

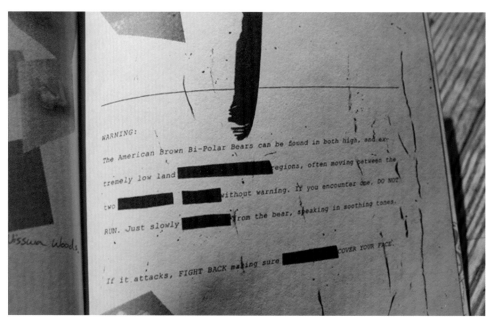

We Heart Poster Art

Series of limited edition prints using minimal and simplistic designs based on 2009/2010 album releases. Printed on 16.5x11.7" recycled Ecostar uncoated paper 150gsm

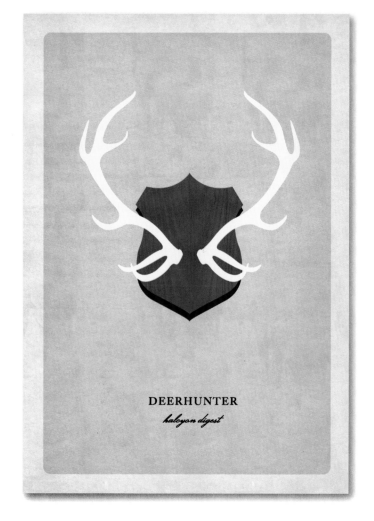

DEERHUNTER

halcyon digest

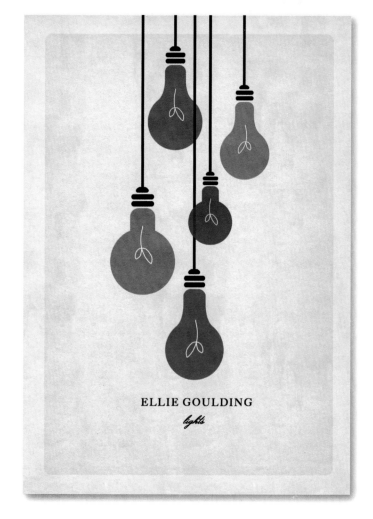

ELLIE GOULDING

lights

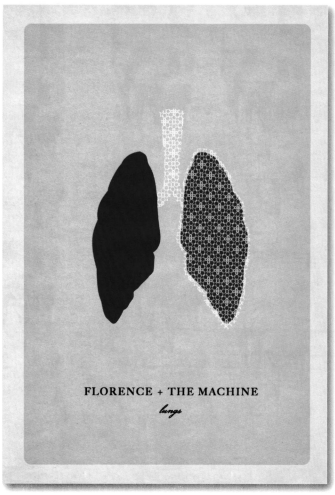

FLORENCE + THE MACHINE

lungs

THE BLACK KEYS

brothers

Bilistic Airbrushing

Business cards for Sydney, Australia based airbrush artist Bilistic. Red foil stamped logo printed on charcoal matte laminate card 350gsm.

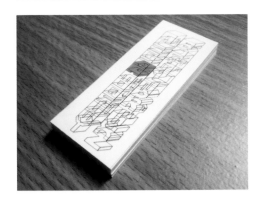

Self-promotion miniature cards for Sydney, Australia based graphic designer, Katerina Vourgos. 14 individual typography designs printed on 28x70mm matte laminate cards.

The Creative Method

Build Your Own

The aim was to create a unique gift to give the studio's own clients at Christmas and to act as a new business introduction. It needed to remind them of who The Creative Method are and the long hours that they put into their work. It needed to feature all of their staff, reflect their creativity and sense of humor. The print run was 5000 labels. They obtained high quality cleanskin wines and created their own labels. Each label was based on one staff member. It included a number of facial features and the clients were encouraged to BYO - Build Their Own.

The wine and the label is the perfect substitute for when the real person cannot be there.

Designer: Andi Yanto
Creative Director: Tony Ibbotson
Artworker: Greg Coles
Client: The Creative Method

The Creative Method

Imaginitol

Description of project: The brief was to create an interesting and engaging invitation to The Creative Method Xmas party. It needed to illustrate what they do but also create a high level of interest and anticipation for the party. It needed to be humorous and memorable. It was also required to work as a new business piece outside of the Christmas invitation.

We based the idea on an imaginary pharmaceutical tablet that would solve their creative issues. Initially they were emailed a doctor's prescription, followed by the package in a discrete paper bag. The invitation and the tablets were located inside. The party included staff dressed as doctors and medicinal shots administered by transvestites. The box and invitation are used as a new business teaser.

Designers: Mayra Monobe and Sinead McDevitt
Creative Director: Tony Ibbotson

The Creative Method Business Cards and Letterhead

To design a series of business cards for The Creative Method. The main goal was to create a 'wow' factor. The cards needed to stand out above those of other design companies, they needed to remind people of who the designers are and what they do.

The best case scenario would be for the cards to create a discussion point around a new business table or for clients to hold onto them to show friends or ultimately other likely clients. The cards needed to reflect the individuality of each of the staff members and be something

that they would want to hand over.

The brief for the letterhead was to follow up on the concept of The Creative Method business cards, which had an image of each staff member changing faces from babies to adults using a lenticular printing technique. The challenge with the letterhead was to translate a similar concept in a similar style that was not as personal, yet reflecting the same idea of changing faces to illustrate idea generation, possibilities and fun. The back of the letterhead literally shows personality by having parts of faces of

different staff members of The Creative Method. The paper can be folded to create different faces with the help of fine perforations. Either amused or happy faces are created every time, illustrating that The Creative Method always keeps its clients happy with a great range of different possibilities. The letterhead always folds down to DL size and can also be cut to make 'with compliments' slips. It is a perfect demonstration of the studio's work & play attitude and a great talking point.

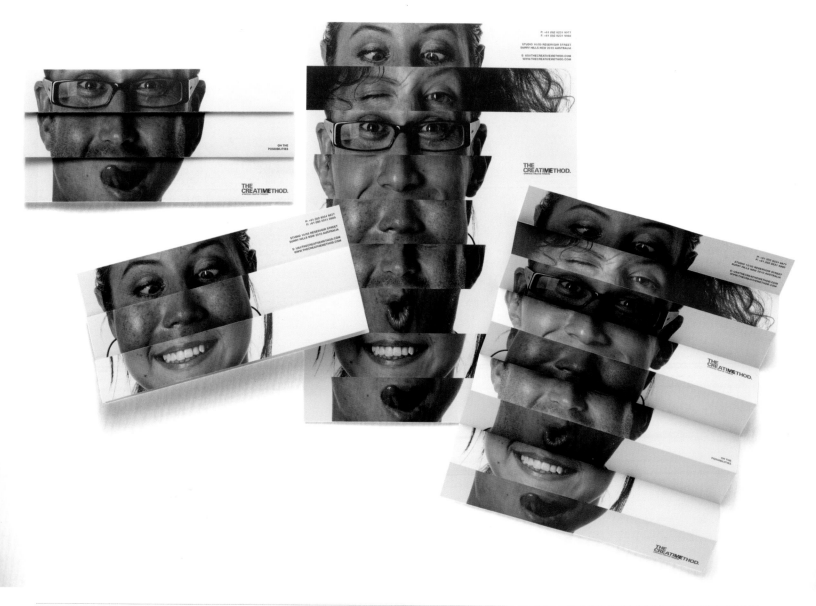

Alongkorn

Alongkorn is a bespoke tailor shop specialized in classic men's clothing in Bangkok. The company is famous for their craft and the variety of fabrics they offer to their customers. They have been in business since 1958. The word "Alongkorn" means "Embellishment" in Thai. They wanted to update the brand and make the idea of custom-made clothing more attractive to the younger generation but without sacrificing the classic designs and the high-level craft quality of the brand. Tnop™ Design explored many directions but focused mainly on creating the logotype for the brand. They looked back at the history of Alongkorn's logos and recreated the new logo based on previous ones. The final logo is based on the hand done pad-stitching that's used in the lining of the suit. It represents the craftsmanship, attention to detail, classic approach and sophistication of the brand. The new identity package for the brand also reflects craftsmanship and sophistication – especially the business card, in the form of tailor's chalk, made of 2 card stock sheets glued together to create an air pocket inside, and embossed on both sides.

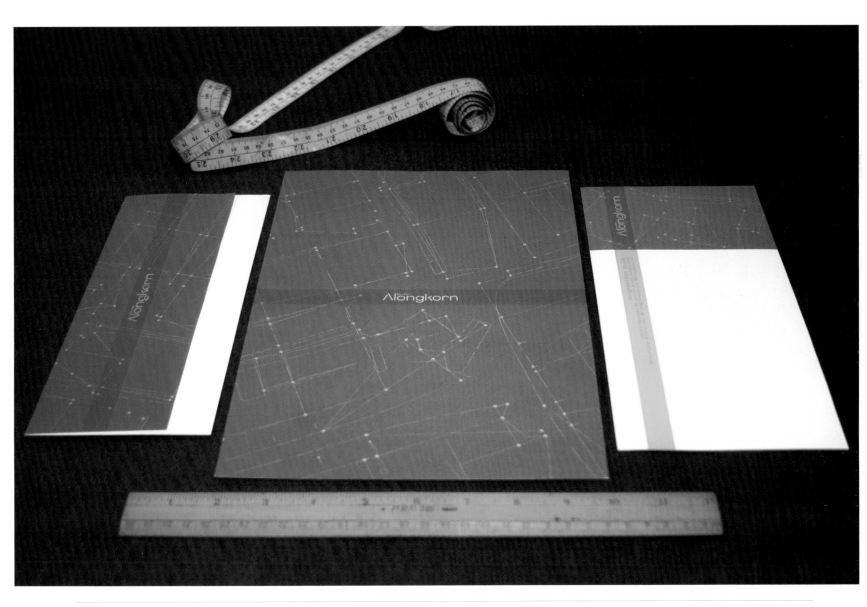

ThreeSevenFive

The ThreeSevenFive business card supports the grid system and narrative nature of the identity.

Sticker created as a promotional piece to showcase layout and typography. In addition, a custom display typeface was created.

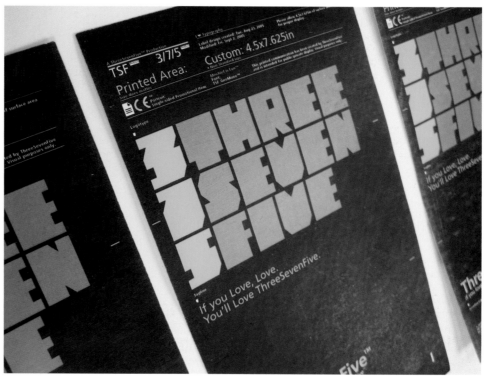

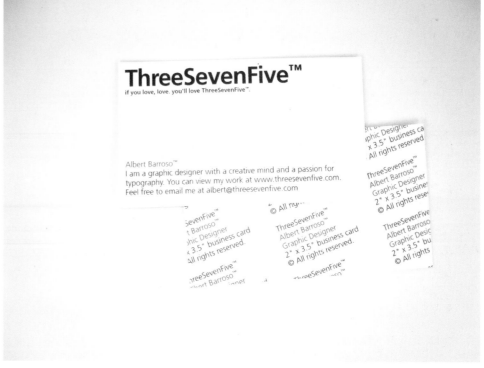

The Sci-Fi London Film Festival commissioned Transmission to raise their public profile, specifically within the arts and music sectors. The designers suggested curating a contemporary art exhibition centered around the theme 'Life In 2050' to be held in a prominent Central London gallery.

Transmission commissioned 22 leading and emerging visual artists from around the world, who had been hand picked for their unique styles and interest in the subject matter. The event was held at the Proud Central Gallery and generated a vast amount of press coverage in international design, illustration and style magazines.

Transmission generated all the press and p.r material for the event, which included organizing a private view which was sponsored by Warp Records and Courvoisier.

Contributors included Alex Trochut, Dan McPharlin, Daniel K. Sparkes, Emiliano Granado, Graham Carter, Hort, Ivan Jones, James Taylor, Jason Tozer, Kerry Roper, Lee Baker, Mario Hugo, MVM, Panda Yoghurt, Universal Everything and Unlimited.

32
THIRTY TWO PER CENT OF THE WORLD'S POPULATION ARE NOW AGED OVER 60.
UNITED NATIONS

15
ONE MILLION HECTARES OF WOODLAND HAVE BEEN PLANTED SINCE 2010, REDUCING CO2 EMISSIONS BY FIFTEEN PER CENT.
FORESTRY COMMISSION, UK

25
TWENTY FIVE PER CENT OF THE WORLD'S ELECTRICITY IS NOW GENERATED BY SOLAR PANELS IN THE DESERT.
GREENPEACE

50
FIFTY PER CENT OF EUROPEAN AMPHIBIANS HAVE BECOME EXTINCT IN THE PAST 40 YEARS.
ZOOLOGICAL SOCIETY, LONDON

70
WORLD WIDE FOOD PRODUCTION HAS INCREASED BY SEVENTY PER CENT OVER 40 YEARS, TO FEED THE GROWING POPULATION.
UNITED NATIONS FOOD AGENCY

05
SPRING TIME IN THE UK LASTS FIVE MONTHS, FROM LATE JANUARY TO LATE JUNE.
ROYAL BOTANICAL GARDENS, EDINBURGH

10
THE PRICE TO BUY AN ANDROID HAS REDUCED BY TEN PER CENT SINCE 2010.
BASED ON THE CURRENT AND PROJECTED PRICE OF THE KOKORO ANDROID

66
SIXTY SIX PER CENT OF THE WORLD'S POPULATION NOW LIVE IN CITIES.
UN-HABITAT

01
THE NUMBER OF WORLD CUP'S WON BY A TEAM OF ROBOTS.
CARLOS III UNIVERSITY, MADRID

71
THE WORLD'S POPULATION HAS RISEN BY SEVENTY ONE PER CENT IN 40 YEARS TO REACH 9 BILLION.
UNITED NATIONS

90
SUNDAY ATTENDANCE AT CHRISTIAN CHURCHES HAS FALLEN BY NINETY PER CENT SINCE 2010.
CHRISTIAN RESEARCH

01
MASSACHUSETTS IS THE ONLY STATE IN THE USA, WHERE IT IS LEGAL TO MARRY A ROBOT.
UNIVERSITY OF MAASTRICHT

Show Below

Show Below is a yearly contemporary art exhibition featuring original work by a collection of Brighton's finest print-makers, illustrators and designers.

Transmission have contributed original poster artwork to each exhibition since it's conception and have also created the branding which includes posters, fliers and website design.

Each year Transmission experiments with typography, colour and composition within the constraints of a poster format. Their images are based on contemporary culture themes, which have included iconic catchphrases and lines from the classic film 'Coming to America'.

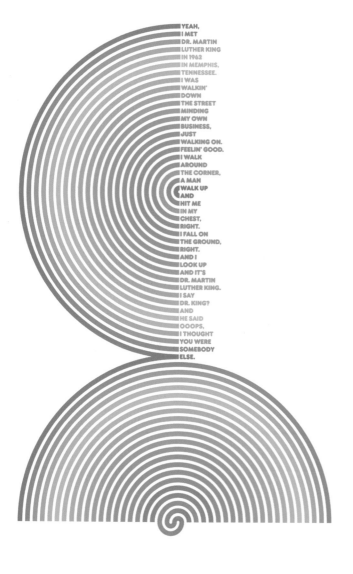

Halle Berry, 2002
Extract from Oscar acceptance speech

HE'S
NOT THE
MESSIAH

HE'S A VERY
NAUGHTY BOY

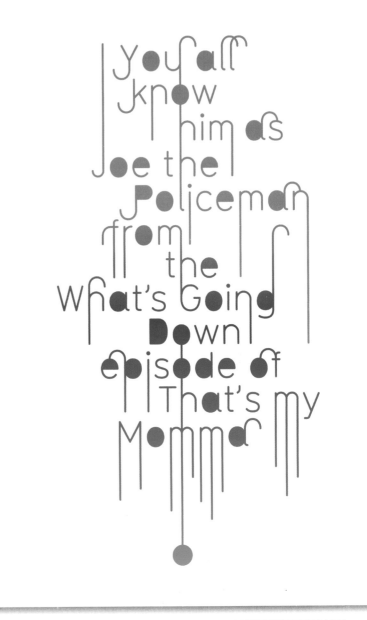

You all
know
him as
Joe the
Policeman
from
the
What's Going
Down
episode of
That's my
Momma

Landing

Design of logo and collaterals for the dance art project Landing 2008 held at St. Olavs Hospital in Trondheim Norway as part of the Landing project – taking the arts to unconventional places.

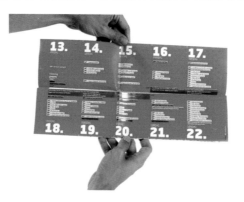

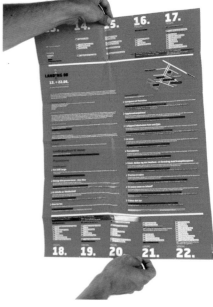

The starting point for the new identity for the MMK, the Museum for Contemporary Art in Frankfurt, was the triangular shape of the building. The triangle and the typographic system of two fonts work as the basic elements of the new corporate design.

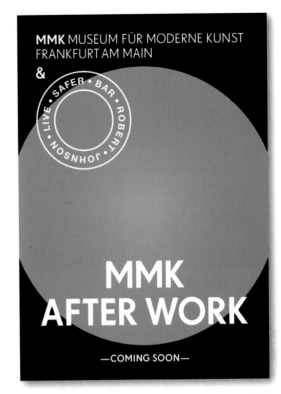

MMK Zollamt

In parallel with redesigning the identity of the MMK, a modern art museum in Frankfurt, Germany, Margaret Warzecha - hauser lacour redesigned the identity of MMK Zollamt, an art project space located within the museum. Taking inspiration from the space's original function as a customhouse, the design of the identity has a heraldic appearance.

Designer Index

Anti

WEB:
www.anti-ink.com
MAIL:
kenneth@anti.as
TEL:
+(47) 934 45 238
ADDRESS:
Kristian Augustsgt. 13, 0164 Oslo, Norway
PAGES:
8-11

Apfel Zeit

WEB:
www.apfelzet.de
MAIL:
contact@apfelzet.de
TEL:
+ 49 (0)30 68 22 48 53
ADDRESS:
Brunnenstraße 7D, 10119 Berlin, Germany
PAGES:
12-19

Asylum

WEB:
www.theasylum.com.sg
MAIL:
info@theasylum.com.sg
TEL:
+ 65 6324 2289
ADDRESS:
69 Circular Road, #03-01, Singapore, 049423
PAGES:
20-21

Atipus

WEB:
www.atipus.com
MAIL:
info@atipus.com
TEL:
+34 93 485 13 95
ADDRESS:
C/ Pallars 85, 1r 2a, 08018 Barcelona, Spain
PAGES:
22-25

Brogen Averill

WEB:
brogenaverill.com
MAIL:
brogen@thingwebsite.com
TEL:
+ 64 (0)21 277 2858
PAGES:
26-27

Edgar Bąk

WEB:
www.edgarbak.info
MAIL:
poczta@edgarbak.info
TEL:
+48 501 128 646
ADDRESS:
ul. Ogrodowa 31/35, 00-893 Warszawa, Poland
PAGES:
28-31

bauer – konzept & gestaltung

WEB:
www.erwinbauer.com
MAIL:
office@erwinbauer.com
TEL:
+43 1 504 48 18 0
ADDRESS:
Weyringerstrasse 36/1, 1040 Vienna, Austria
PAGES:
32-37

Boccalatte

WEB:
boccalatte.com
MAIL:
hello@boccalatte.com
TEL:
+61 2 9211 9411
PAGES:
38-41

Mark Brooks

WEB:
www.markbrooksgraphikdesign.com
MAIL:
contact@mark.brooks.name
TEL:
+34 644 468 319
ADDRESS:
Via Laietana, 64, Principal,
08003 Barcelona, Spain
PAGES:
42-45

Büro North

WEB:
www.buronorth.com
MAIL:
reception@buronorth.com
TEL:
+613 9654 3259
ADDRESS:
Level 1 / 35 Little Bourke Street
Melbourne, VIC 3000 Australia
PAGES:
46-49

Chen Design Associates

WEB:
www.chendesign.com
MAIL:
info@chendesign.com
TEL:
+1 415 896 5338
ADDRESS:
632 Commercial Street Fifth Floor
San Francisco, CA 94111-2599, USA
PAGES:
50-51

Chris Clarke

WEB:
www.chris-clarke.co.uk
MAIL:
mail@chris-clarke.co.uk
TEL:
+44 (0)7845 629 816
ADDRESS:
Unit 47, SODA studios
London, E8 4DG, UK
PAGES:
52-53

COOEE

WEB:
cooee.nl
MAIL:
leon@cooee.nl
TEL:
+31 (0)6 183 972 97
ADDRESS:
Zuideinde 296
1035 PM Amsterdam, The Netherlands
PAGES:
54-56

Ina Cotsou

WEB:
www.inacotsou.com
MAIL:
mail@inacotsou.com
TEL:
+49 30 49 500 402
PAGES:
58-59

Dalston Creative

WEB:
www.dalston.se
MAIL:
info@dalston.se
TEL:
+46 (0)76 028 20 51
ADDRESS:
Nybrogatan 34, 3tr, 114 39 Stockholm, Sweden
PAGES:
50-53

Detail

WEB:
www.detail.ie
MAIL:
mail@detail.ie
TEL:
+353 1 878 3168
ADDRESS:
11 The Friary, Bow Street, Smithfield,
Dublin 7, Ireland
PAGES:
64-67

Joshua Distler

WEB:
www.joshuadistler.com
MAIL:
josh@joshuadistler.com
PAGES:
57, 68-69

Elixir Design

WEB:
www.elixirdesign.com
MAIL:
info@elixirdesign.com
TEL:
+ 1 415 834 0300
ADDRESS:
2134 Van Ness Avenue
San Francisco, CA 94102, USA
PAGES:
70-71

Calle Enstrom

WEB:
www.calleenstrom.se
MAIL:
calle@calleenstrom.se
PAGES:
72-73

Evenson Design Group

WEB:
www.evensondesign.com
MAIL:
sevenson@evensondesign.com
TEL:
+1 310 204 1995
ADDRESS:
4445 Overland Ave.
Culver City, CA 90230, USA
PAGES:
74

Faust

WEB:
www.faustltd.com
MAIL:
info@faustltd.com
TEL:
+1 708 447 0608
ADDRESS:
217 Millbridge Road
Riverside, Illinois 60546, USA
PAGES:
75-77

Fridge Creative

WEB:
www.fridgecreative.co.uk
MAIL:
hello@fridgecreative.co.uk
TEL:
+44 (0) 20 7729 8661
ADDRESS:
59 Charlotte Road, Hoxton
London EC2A 3QT, United Kingdom
PAGES:
78-79

Funnel

WEB:
www.funnel.tv
MAIL:
eric@funnel.tv
TEL:
+1 317 590 5355
PAGES:
80-85

gdloft

WEB:
www.gdloft.com
MAIL:
phl@gdloft.com
PAGES:
86-91

Golden Cosmos

WEB:
www.golden-cosmos.com
MAIL:
doris@golden-cosmos.com
PAGES:
92-93

Anna Härlin

WEB:
www.annahaerlin.de
MAIL:
anna@annahaerlin.de
ADDRESS:
Oderberger Str. 53, 10435 Berlin, Germany
PAGES:
94-97

Alberto Hernández

WEB:
hereigo.co.uk
MAIL:
alberto@hereigo.co.uk
TEL:
+44 (0)75 1656 1613
PAGES:
98-103

Heydays

WEB:
www.heydays.info
MAIL:
hey@heydays.info
TEL:
(+47) 905 19 260
PAGES:
104-111

HI(NY)

WEB:
www.hinydesign.com
MAIL:
info@hinydesign.com
TEL:
+1 646 808 0708
ADDRESS:
401 Broadway Suite 1908
New York, NY 10013, USA
PAGES:
112

Hype & Slippers

WEB:
www.hypeandslippers.com
MAIL:
hello@hypeandslippers.com
TEL:
+44 (0) 117 325 1160
ADDRESS:
Bristol & Exeter House, Lower Approach Road,
Temple Meads, Bristol, BS1 6QS, UK
PAGES:
114-115

Hyperakt

WEB:
www.hyperakt.com
MAIL:
whatsup@hyperakt.com
TEL:
+1 718 855 4250
ADDRESS:
401 Smith Street, Brooklyn, NY, 11231, USA
PAGES:
116-117

Ideo Comunicadores

WEB:
www.ideo.com.pe
MAIL:
daniela@ideo.com.pe
ADDRESS:
Av. Reducto 864 of. 1502, Miraflores, Lima, Peru
PAGES:
118-119

James Kape

WEB:
www.jameskape.com
MAIL:
ail@jameskape.com
TEL:
+ 1(347) 369 3966
PAGES:
113, 120-121

L2M3 Kommunikationsdesign GmbH

WEB:
www.l2m3.com
MAIL:
info@l2m3.com
TEL:
+ 49 (0)711.99 33 91 60
ADDRESS:
Hölderlinstrasse 57
70193 Stuttgart, Germany
PAGES:
122-127

Lava

WEB:
www.lava.nl
MAIL:
info @lava.nl
TEL:
+31 20 6222640
ADDRESS:
Silodam 1F
1013 Al Amsterdam, the Netherlands
PAGES:
128-129

Loose Collective - Graham Jones

WEB:
loosecollective.blogspot.com
MAIL:
gman@loosecollective.net
TEL:
+44 (0)773 275 2698
ADDRESS:
Flat 38, Goodhope Mill
Ashton-U-Lyne, Manchester, OL6 7SB, UK
PAGES:
130-137

Lundgren+Lindqvist

WEB:
www.lundgrenlindqvist.se
MAIL:
hello@lundgrenlindqvist.se
TEL:
+46 (0) 736 90 90 11
ADDRESS:
Karl Johansgatan 72
SE-414 55 Gothenburg, Sweden
PAGES:
138-147

Method

WEB:
method.com
MAIL:
inquiries@method.com
PAGES:
148-149

milchhof:atelier

WEB:
www.milchhof.net
MAIL:
post@milchhof.net
TEL:
+49 (0)30 44052612
ADDRESS:
Kastanienallee 73, 10435 Berlin, Germany
PAGES:
150-151

Mind Design

WEB:
www.minddesign.co.uk
MAIL:
info@minddesign.co.uk
TEL:
+44 (0)20 7254 2114
ADDRESS:
Unit 33A, Regents Studios
8 Andrews Road, London E8 4QN, United Kingdom
PAGES:
152-153

Mission Design

WEB:
www.mission.no
MAIL:
hello@mission.no
ADDRESS:
Henrik Ibsen Gate 100
0230 Oslo, Norway
PAGES:
154-159

Moving Brands

WEB:
www.movingbrands.com
MAIL:
info@movingbrands.com
TEL:
+44 (0) 20 7739 7700
PAGES:
160-161

MyORB

WEB:
www.myorangebox.com
MAIL:
hello@myorangebox.com
TEL:
+1 212 226 4216
ADDRESS:
241 Centre Street 4th floor, New York, NY 10013, USA
PAGES:
162-169

Niessen & de Vries

WEB:
www.niessendevries.nl
MAIL:
info@niessendevries.nl
TEL:
+31(0)20 66 33 323
PAGES:
170-175

Official Classic

WEB:
www.officialclassic.com
MAIL:
info@officialclassic.com
TEL:
+ 14534779-2-42
ADDRESS:
Adria setany, 5/A, 1148 Budapest, Hungary
PAGES:
176-181

onlab

WEB:
www.onlab.ch
TEL:
+49 (0)30 80 61 58 80
ADDRESS:
Oderberger Straße 11
10435 Berlin, Germany
PAGES:
182-183

Operation Butterfly

WEB:
www.operationbutterfly.com
MAIL:
contact@operationbutterfly.com
TEL:
+49 69 27 13 99 63
ADDRESS:
Kaiserstraße 61 D-60329, Frankfurt am Main,
Germany
PAGES:
184-187

Cody Paulson

WEB:
cargocollective.com/codypaulson
MAIL:
cody@swimcreative.com
ADDRESS:
415 E Superior St
Duluth, MN 55802, USA
PAGES:
185

Mads Jakob Poulsen

WEB:
www.madsjakobpoulsen.dk
MAIL:
hello@madsjakobpoulsen.dk
PAGES:
188-189

Praline

WEB:
www.designbypraline.com
MAIL:
info@designbypraline.com
TEL:
+44 (0)20 7503 4019
ADDRESS:
14 Quebec Wharf
315 Kingsland Road, London E8 4DJ, UK
PAGES:
190-197

Raffinerie

WEB:
www.raffinerie.com
MAIL:
contact@raffinerie.com
TEL:
+41 (0) 43 322 11 11
ADDRESS:
Anwandstrasse 62
8004 Zürich, Switzerland
PAGES:
198-201

Range

WEB:
www.rangeus.com
TEL:
+1 214 744 0555
ADDRESS:
2257 Vantage Street
Dallas, Texas 75207, USA
PAGES:
202-204

Red Organic

WEB:
www.redorganic.com
MAIL:
aurora@redorganic.com
PAGES:
205

Janine Rewell - Lotta Nieminen

WEB:
www.janinerewell.com
MAIL:
janine@janinerewell.com
TEL:
+358 44 319 0586
PAGES:
206-207

Roycroft Design

WEB:
www.roycroftdesign.com
MAIL:
info@roycroftdesign.com
TEL:
+1 617 720 4506
ADDRESS:
184 High Street, Suite 501
Boston, MA 02110, USA
PAGES:
208

Sawdust

WEB:
www.madebysawdust.co.uk
MAIL:
studio@madebysawdust.co.uk
TEL:
+44 (0) 20 7739 9787
ADDRESS:
Unit 2.04, 12–18 Hoxton Street
London N1 6NG, United Kingdom
PAGES:
209-211

Sign*

WEB:
www.designbysign.com
MAIL:
info@designbysign.com
TEL:
+32 2 218 20 70
ADDRESS:
57, Rue Locquenghien
1000 Brussels, Belgium
PAGES:
212

Robert Sitek

WEB:
www.behance.net/robertsitek
PAGES:
213

Spunk Design Machine

WEB:
spkdm.com
MAIL:
info@spkdm.com
TEL:
+1 612 724 3444
ADDRESS:
4933 34th Ave S
Minneapolis MN 55417, USA
PAGES:
214-215

Anke Stohlmann Design

WEB:
www.ankestohlmanndesign.com
MAIL:
info@ankestohlmanndesign.com
TEL:
+1 646 808 0691
PAGES:
216

Studio Brave

WEB:
studiobrave.com.au
MAIL:
info@studiobrave.com.au
ADDRESS:
Level 5, 289 Flinders Lane
Melbourne VIC 3000, Australia
PAGES:
217-221

StudioConover

WEB:
www.studioconover.com
MAIL:
buildingcontexture@studioconover.com
TEL:
+1 619 238 1999
ADDRESS:
800 West Ivy Street, Studio C
San Diego, CA 92101, USA
PAGES:
222-223

Studio On Fire

WEB:
www.studioonfire.com
MAIL:
info@studioonfire.com
TEL:
+1 612 379 3000
ADDRESS:
1621 East Hennepin Avenue #B10
Minneapolis, Minnesota 55414, USA
PAGES:
224-225

Surgery7

WEB:
www.surgeryseven.com
MAIL:
hello@surgeryseven.com
PAGES:
226-231

The Creative Method

WEB:
www.thecreativemethod.com
MAIL:
mail@thecreativemethod.com
TEL:
+61 02 8231 9977
ADDRESS:
Studio 10, Level 4 50 Reservoir St.
Surry Hills, NSW 2010, Australia
PAGES:
232-237

ThreeSevenFive

WEB:
www.threesevenfive.com
MAIL:
albert@threesevenfive.com
PAGES:
240

TNOP™

WEB:
tnop.com
MAIL:
info@tnop.com
TEL:
+1 312 235 0170
ADDRESS:
1440 S Michigan Ave #322
Chicago IL 60605-2956, USA
PAGES:
238-239

Transmission

WEB:
www.thisistransmission.com
MAIL:
lynn@thisistransmission.com
TEL:
+44 (0) 1273 726909
ADDRESS:
Second floor studios, 53 Church road,
Brighton & Hove, BN3 2BD, UK
PAGES:
241-243

upstruct

WEB:
www.upstruct.com
MAIL:
mail@upstruct.com
TEL:
+49 30 702 207 78
ADDRESS:
Alexandrinenstraße 4, 10969, Berlin, Germany
PAGES:
244-245

Margaret Warzecha

WEB:
www.margaretwarzecha.com
MAIL:
info@margaretwarzecha.com
PAGES:
246-249